THE JESUS AGENDA

―――――◆―――――

Rev A. Munro
MA, BD, PHD

Copyright © Andrew Munro 2017
This book is sold subject to the condition that it shall not, by way of trade or otherwise, be lent, resold, hired out, or otherwise circulated without the publisher's prior consent in any form of binding or cover other than that in which it is published and without a similar condition including this condition being imposed on the subsequent publisher.
The moral right of Andrew Munro has been asserted.
ISBN-13: 978-1544260495
ISBN-10: 1544260490

This book has not been created to be specific to any individual's or organizations' situation or needs. Every effort has been made to make this book as accurate as possible. This book should serve only as a general guide and not as the ultimate source of subject information. This book contains information that might be dated and is intended only to educate and entertain. The author shall have no liability or responsibility to any person or entity regarding any loss or damage incurred, or alleged to have incurred, directly or indirectly, by the information contained in this book.

CONTENTS

Acknowledgments .... *i*
1. *"And he was put in a coffin in Egypt."* *3*
2. *"And throwing off his mantle he sprang up and came to Jesus."* . *9*
3. *"And what does the Lord require of you."* *14*
4. *"Blessed are the poor in spirit, theirs is the Kingdom of Heaven." 20*
5. *"But a Samaritan had compassion."* *25*
6. *"But I will be with you."* *30*
7. *"Commit your way to the Lord, trust in Him and He will act.". 36*
8. *"Do Whatever He Tells You."* *42*
9. *"Everyone who exalts himself will be humbled but he who humbles himself will be exalted."* *47*
10. *"For he has made known to us in all wisdom and insight the mystery of his will according to his purpose which he set forth in Christ."* *52*
11. *"He noticed how full of idols he city was."* *58*
12. *"He taught as one who had Authority, not as the Scribes."* *64*
13. *"He was a man of mighty valour, but he was a leper."* *73*
14. *"I establish my covenant with you."* *78*
15. *"Jesus closed the book."* *84*
16. *"Let this mind be in you which was also in Christ Jesus."* *89*
17. *"Let us go with you for we have heard that God is with you." 94*
18. *"Let your light so shine before men, that they may see your good works and give glory to your father who is in Heaven."* *99*
19. *"Lord teach us to pray as John taught his disciples."* *107*
20. *"Now there are variations of gifts but the same Spirit."* *115*
21. *"That Peter's shadow might fall on them."* *121*
22. *"The Chariots of Israel and its horsemen."* *127*

23. "The greatest of these is Love." 132
24. "The righteousness of the righteous shall not believe him when he transgresses and as for the wickedness of the wicked, he shall not fall by it when he turns from his wickedness." 139
25. "Trade with these till I come." 145
26. "What is man that thou art mindful of him?" 149
27. "He is not here, for he has risen as he said." 154
28. "Not everyone who says to me, 'Lord, Lord' shall enter the Kingdom of Heaven, but he who does the will of my Father who is in heaven." 161

ACKNOWLEDGMENTS

Acknowledgement is duly and thankfully made for all quotations, particularly to the Daily Mail for the article "Farewell fit for a hero" by Snejana Farberov.

Biblical quotations are from the Revised Standard Version with two exceptions.

On my tenth birthday my grandparents gave me a Bible as a present. It made me feel very grown up and very important. I have chosen to use the Authorised Version to say a belated thanks to them.

A special thanks is accorded to Mrs Rita Davy for turning my scrawl into legible typing, and to my granddaughter Lorraine for her computer expertise.

Many people have suggested to Dr Munro that he should publish his sermons as they have much to offer.

Dr Munro is a Church of Scotland minister ordained over forty years ago. He has an honours MA in philosophy, a first-class honours BD, and Fellowship in theology in Glasgow University. In addition to his degree and fellowship, the prestigious preaching prize was awarded to him. He studied at the universities of Glasgow, Aberdeen and Tübingen (the latter with Professors Moltmann, Ebeling and Oberman). He also has a postgraduate certificate in religious education. He has taught theology in a college at Ghana University and has taught in two major Scottish secondary schools. He has also been adviser in religious education in Dumfries & Galloway, responsible for pupils from nursery to school leaving at eighteen. He served on the committee which negotiated and produced the scheme of examinations in all Scottish schools.

He has served as a parish minister and took the role of preaching very seriously. It concerns him a great deal that many people see the Christian faith as primarily a matter of believing the unbelievable, and sought by his preaching to interpret the Gospels in such a way that our modern 'scientific' society does not reject them for the wrong reasons.

Accordingly, he has put together a group of sermons which illustrate this concern.

KW

*

It will be recognised that the following are written as sermons and not as narrative English.

AM

GENESIS 50: 15-26

15. When Joseph's brothers saw that their father was dead, they said, "It may be that Joseph will hate us and pay us back for all the evil which we did to him."

16. So they sent a message to Joseph, saying, "Your father gave this command before he died,

17. 'Say to Joseph, Forgive, I pray you, the transgression of your brothers and their sin, because they did evil to you.' And now, we pray you, forgive the transgression of the servants of the God of your father." Joseph wept when they spoke to him.

18. His brothers also came and fell down before him, and said, "Behold, we are your servants."

19. But Joseph said to them, "Fear not, for am I in the place of God?

20. As for you, you meant evil against me; but God meant it for good, to bring it about that many people should be kept alive, as they are today.

21. So do not fear; I will provide for you and your little ones." Thus he reassured them and comforted them.

22. So Joseph dwelt in Egypt, he and his father's house; and Joseph lived a hundred and ten years.

23. And Joseph saw E'phraim's children of the third generation; the children also of Machir the son of Manas'seh were born upon Joseph's knees.

24. And Joseph said to his brothers, "I am about to die; but God will visit you, and bring you up out of this land to the land which he swore to Abraham, to Isaac, and to Jacob."

25. Then Joseph took an oath of the sons of Israel, saying, "God will visit you, and you shall carry up my bones from here."

26. So Joseph died, being a hundred and ten years old; and they embalmed him, and he was put in a coffin in Egypt.

1.

"And he was put in a coffin in Egypt."

I remember as a student having an opportunity to visit the French Protestant monastery at Taizé. It was a wonderful experience and I still from time to time listen to the monks chanting (on the tape I brought home). It was a holy place and to this day has become a centre for pilgrimage and people are reminded of the need for reconciliation between the nations – and Roger Schutz, the founder, made it his joy to bring together young people from all nations. (Roger Schutz was, alas, murdered by a "pilgrim" who resented his message and coincidentally he also had the ecumenical honour of being a Protestant Pastor who received Holy Communion from the Pope).

On my visit there was a Presbyterian minister who had come to Taizé to get peace and quiet to finish his thesis. In return for his hospitality he was asked to do the morning prayers which consisted of a Bible reading and words of commentary. The readings were from the book of Nehemiah and Chapter 10 v 1-26 is simply a list of names. It was quite an experience to sit and watch the monks trying to contain their giggles at the thought that he was going to have to make a sermon out of this. But he soon had them quiet – not because he was a great preacher – but because he'd done his homework and brought out of this most unpromising passage the message that even those who only played a minor part still had their names numbered in God's kingdom.

At first sight our text here is one that could make the monks want to giggle, "He was put in a coffin in Egypt." Joseph, the slave turned Prime Minister, ended his earthy life in the country he'd served so well but in which he was still a foreigner. It was a long life and an eventful one. It was also a remarkable story of a life of faith. In all that happened to Joseph, all the dramatic incidents – all the let-downs, we never once hear a complaint or even a questioning. Joseph wasn't one of those characters who asked, "Why did God let this happen to me?" Equally, however, he was not a resigner. Out of each situation he emerged not just making the best of a bad job, but triumphing over his circumstances – and the reason is simple. His relationship with God was right – his life was an illustration of what St Paul was many years later to say. "I have learned, whatever state that I am in, therewith to be content."

We meet Joseph first as a teenager and he exhibits all the immaturity we expect. He was what we call in Scotland "a lad o' pairts" (a boy of ability). In this ability he outstripped his family but he was immature enough not to anticipate a hostile reaction. He paraded his cleverness in a way that led to jealousy, and we all know how his brothers took their revenge – by selling him into slavery. Here there is no mention of fear or homesickness but a quick assertion of his ability and rise to a position of responsibility.

We read too of how he attracted the amorous attentions of Potiphar's wife, which with wisdom that shows his growing maturity, he resists and in the by going exhibits a maturity beyond his generation. The old saying "Hell has no fury like a woman scorned" applies here and Joseph has to bear this fury. He suffers the indignity of prison and remember, it's prison in a foreign land. But again there's no mentioning of any resentment or questioning. Joseph treats the prison experience like any other and uses it to further discourse that even in a foreign gaol God is still to be found. You'll remember the incident with Pharaoh's butler. Joseph befriended him in prison and he promised to bring his plight to Pharaoh on his release – and promptly forgot, leaving Joseph languishing another two years in gaol. These are a series of carefully selected stories to show the extent of Joseph's unhappy experiences: his own family exiled him, a total stranger falsely libelled him and had him falsely imprisoned, a friend he helped forgot him. Most of us having even one of these experiences would be embittered. But not Joseph.

George MacDonald, the Victorian children's novelist, tells of a lady feeling let down and resentful. "I wish I'd never been made," she cried.

To which her friend replied, "My dear you're not made yet, you're only being made and you're quarrelling with the Maker's process."

How many of us quarrel with the Maker's process and nurse our wrath instead of helping him to help us grow?

Joseph helped his Maker's process and look at the result. We meet at the end of the Bible's first book a spirit unparalleled until we meet Jesus in the Gospels. It was Jesus who said, "Judge not that ye be not judged."

Joseph, in reply to his brothers, said, "Am I in the place of God?"

It's a delicious little bit of Scripture, this. Joseph knew his brothers were lying through their teeth with this story about Jacob craving his forgiveness. They had not changed: they had resisted the Maker's process! But still Joseph judged not and even if we rule out something as naive as retaliation and revenge, it would have been no surprise if Joseph had said to his brothers, "Oh I forgive you – now get out of here." But instead he assumed the responsibility for them – this is the forgiving and going the extra mile that Jesus taught. This is the universal truth of the Gospel – whenever someone truly co-operates with the Maker's process they end up being Christlike, whatever their culture – whatever their generation – whatever their creed. The true test of orthodoxy is not the ability to forgive and deal with life's experience without succumbing to bitterness, and learn the lesson that if we let God, even out of the greatest tragedy, He can bring the works of love.

"And he was put in a coffin in Egypt." A seemingly strange conclusion for the first book of the Bible. Incomplete – Joseph wasn't buried – but nothing is missed out, no last verses have been lost. He was put in a coffin in Egypt. Bishop Leighton of the seventeenth century took seriously the idea of life as being in God's process and preached that we should all die in an Inn – representing the idea that we were only resting on a journey. (By a quirk of faith the good bishop did so die!) The author of Genesis concluded with the same point. Joseph had no last resting place – he had a coffin but no grave – the Maker's process had only finished stage one with Joseph! So, what seemed an unpromising text is actually a great cry of hope – even in death – as Jesus too taught us – God has not completed us yet!

MARK 10: 46-52

46. And they came to Jericho; and as he was leaving Jericho with his disciples and a great multitude, Bartimae'us, a blind beggar, the son of Timae'us, was sitting by the roadside.

47. And when he heard that it was Jesus of Nazareth, he began to cry out and say, "Jesus, Son of David, have mercy on me!"

48. And many rebuked him, telling him to be silent; but he cried out all the more, "Son of David, have mercy on me!"

49. And Jesus stopped and said, "Call him." And they called the blind man, saying to him, "Take heart; rise, he is calling you."

50. And throwing off his mantle he sprang up and came to Jesus.

51. And Jesus said to him, "What do you want me to do for you?" And the blind man said to him, "Master, let me receive my sight."

52. And Jesus said to him, "Go your way; your faith has made you well." And immediately he received his sight and followed him on the way.

2.

"And throwing off his mantle he sprang up and came to Jesus."

O little luxury don't you cry
You'll be a necessity, by and by.

I cannot remember where I heard that rhyme or what introduced me to it. But it tells us a lot about ourselves. If we compare our lifestyles with that of our grandparents we inevitably think of things that are essential – we couldn't imagine life without them – and yet our grandparents not only lived without them but didn't know about them. What about a video recorder? Or a microwave? Or a laptop? And along with these items and many more we could list, has come a bit of confusion – what is a need and what is a want? Most of these items have cost consequences both in their purchase price and running costs. We have come to think in our modern world of things that we NEED which other generations were happy without. And even more so if we compare our living pattern with our fellow humans in the so-called third world. It really is quite a salutary exercise for us to think through what we need and what we want. If we have more wants than needs then we won't be very happy and we could live an incomplete life trying to meet all our wants.

We can learn quite a bit about this in the story of blind Bartimaeus. Bartimaeus was a beggar and he was a beggar on the road from Jericho to Jerusalem. It was regarded as a plum position – on a trade route between two prosperous cities – and it was likely that a good many well-off traders would take this route, that is, people who could afford to be generous. Also, it was on a pilgrimage route and again the likelihood was that pious pilgrims would feel the need to give alms. So Bartimaeus in all probability would have his wants well taken care of. Not all beggars were poor. But he had a need – he was blind. I'm often asked why God allows so much illness and suffering in the world. In fact, when you think of it, although some people suffer greatly, most of us get through life relatively unscathed – and yet how often it is that a setback, an affliction, or whatever it is, sharpens our insight and awakens us to the difference between needs and wants. Maybe we ought to be wondering why God seems to keep suffering to a minimum! In the case of Bartimaeus it was his blindness that made him aware of what a true need is. The crowd wanted to see what Jesus would be up to next; they wanted to move Bartimaeus down and not spoil the spectacle. But because he had a need he persisted and that takes courage.

A crowd has a kind of personality of its own. There's a kind of subconscious identity. I attended university at a time when all the men wore sports jackets and flannels – now they all wear denim jeans and baggy jumpers. We all fitted in. In modern times lifestyles show that the Church and its teachings are not very prominent. Our wants are supplied and we don't need the Church or a Christian lifestyle. Bartimaeus, because he experienced the difference between need and want, was willing and able to defy the crowd.

An interesting point to notice is how Bartimaeus addresses Jesus. He calls him "son of David". I don't know if you have ever paused to think how many titles were used for Jesus. 'Son of God' – 'Son of Man' – 'Messiah' – 'Lamb of God'. But Bartimaeus chose "Son of David". Now each of these titles has a history and is worthy of a study by itself. Of all these titles, strangely "Son of David" is the most warlike. David was the warrior king who slew his enemies and captured Jerusalem. Given that in this story Jesus is going to Jerusalem to face the prospect of crucifixion, "Lamb of God" would seem the better title. This seems to be quite subtle. St Mark was telling this story to make us think and we could just take from this odd choice of title something very encouraging, namely even an infelicitous use of the wrong title, i.e. a less than full recognition of who Jesus really is – that is enough for Jesus to work on. Strict orthodoxy is not the issue. Jesus can accommodate those who only knew in part.

When he was called, Bartinmaeus responded urgently and without condition. How different from other questioners we meet in the Gospels. Some have not experienced a deep need. "Let me first go and bury my father." Jesus was not callous here. What he was hearing is, "I have duties that are more important." And the saddest one of all, the so-called rich young ruler who "went away sorrowful because he was very rich." I find it hard to see any passage in the Gospels sadder than that.

You can't say that of Bartimaeus – in fact it's the opposite. After his unconventional response we are told "he followed Jesus in the way." In the Gospel context this is ambiguous. We can read it as meaning he followed Jesus to Jerusalem. But also, early Christians were called "followers of the way". It could mean Bartimaeus became one of the Christian faithful. Of course, it also could mean both! It doesn't matter. Bartimaeus is the example of one who could distinguish between need and want and he knew the only response he could make was that of thankful fidelity.

Jesus, on his way to Jerusalem to die, surely had his mind preoccupied with what he had so vividly foretold to his disciples – yet we're told he had time to stop and bring light where there was darkness. If we take our needs to him we will meet the same response – but make sure it is a need – and not a want!

MICAH 6: 1-8

1. Hear what the Lord says: Arise, plead your case before the mountains, and let the hills hear your voice.

2. Hear, you mountains, the controversy of the Lord, and you enduring foundations of the earth; for the Lord has a controversy with his people, and he will contend with Israel.

3. "O my people, what have I done to you? In what have I wearied you? Answer me!

4. For I brought you up from the land of Egypt, and redeemed you from the house of bondage; and I sent before you Moses, Aaron, and Miriam.

5. O my people, remember what Balak king of Moab devised, and what Balaam the son of Be'or answered him, and what happened from Shittim to Gilgal, that you may know the saving acts of the Lord."

6. "With what shall I come before the Lord, and bow myself before God on high? Shall I come before him with burnt offerings, with calves a year old?

7. Will the Lord be pleased with thousands of rams, with ten thousands of rivers of oil? Shall I give my first-born for my transgression, the fruit of my body for the sin of my soul?"

8. He has showed you, O man, what is good; and what does the Lord require of you but to do justice, and to love kindness, and to walk humbly with your God?

3.
"And what does the Lord require of you."

An old gentleman I used to visit fairly regularly never failed to tell me that he had won the scripture prize at school – he had a certificate to prove it. "For Excellence in Bible Knowledge." And he always asked me what Sunday's sermon was about. Usually we had a little discussion about it – and I have to be honest and admit that some of his insights made me wish I had used them. Then he would ask what next Sunday's sermon would be and on one occasion I told him I was using the book of Micah. Despite his Bible certificate he told me he knew nothing about the book of Micah. I suggested to him that he really did know something; in fact most people know at least two things from the book. It was Micah who said "they shall beat their swords into ploughshares and study war no more." And there is the passage that is read in churches all over the world in the Christmas season "But you O Bethlehem Ephrathah who are little to be among the clans of Judah, from you shall come forth for me one who is to be ruler in Israel." Not so well known but very important is the last verse of the book, "Thou wilt show faithfulness to Jacob and steadfast love to Abraham, as thou has sworn to our fathers from the days of old." This is the verse that is read every year at the close of the festival of the day of atonement. It is a reminder of the nation's reliance on God's promises.

There is an important point to be made here about Micah's reference to Bethlehem. This is not saying that Micah had some special gift that enabled him to predict an event that would not occur for another six hundred years. Rather, Micah is saying "the kind of leader we want is someone like David, who was born in Bethlehem. David was far from perfect and his weaknesses are not hidden in the Old Testament. But David acknowledged his failures and fully repented and tried again to live in God's way." This is an important point – the more so in our modern world. It is my experience that open-minded people of our generation are put off having faith because they think they are being asked to believe too many incredulous things. The world of Micah and of the Bible was no different from our world. So when we find that the Biblical generations have a different way of expressing themselves than we have, our task is not to run away in disbelief, but to ask what they meant. And in this way we actually get a richer understanding.

What Micah learned from history, like most profound things, was quite simple – There is a way of living that pleases God and is right, and, a way of living that is not acceptable to God and is wrong. There is a simplistic logic at work here which is as valid today as when Micah taught it. If you copy the way that the pagans live you'll end up being like one of them! He expresses this by predicting conquest by one of the large neighbouring foreign powers. His meaning is clear – what Israel stands for – the covenant with God: the rule of law under God. These will be lost and in their place will come ceremonial which is merely show: has no depth, and corruption will replace morality and acknowledgement of our sinfulness and need of forgiveness will be lost. The richer you become the bigger show you can put on, but, at the price of spiritual growth. Right and wrong is determined not by truth, but by the cleverness of your advocate. Just look around at our society today – don't ever say that Micah is out of date! It can be expressed in his three insights.

a) Do justly – justice need not be a complex idea for people like lawyers and barristers but it is something meant for you and I TO DO! Oxfam shops sell Nicaraguan coffee and the coffee growers benefit. But, what about fancy trainers with a prestigious label and fancy price? The third-world labourer gets ten pence! DO JUSTICE finds its challenge here – we have much to learn.

b) Love mercy. If the prophets merely spoke of doing justice – let's be honest – we would all be condemned in one way or another. Time and again God shows us more than justice; he treats us with mercy. In the Old Testament there are many words for mercy and the one that captures the meaning best is RACHAM – we can translate that as "treat others as someone who came from your womb". In other words, like your child. You don't need me to tell you that the world would be a better place if that were so. But equally we ask what mercy is for our publicly well-known personalities now languishing in prison for their unmerciful abuse of children, whose lives have been forever tainted by their indiscipline and disgust. How often we hear a victim of such behaviour saying they feel they have not received justice. We have to accept that some behaviours are so abhorrent that justice is difficult to attain – loving mercy surely also means that we should try to live in a way that we do not ruin the lives of others – we should ask ourselves – is this a merciful way to behave?

c) Walk humbly before God. Humility is the antidote to pride and pride is the root of most of our troubles. It is pride that makes me think of myself and my self-importance that results in me treating others wrongly: pride makes me less than willing to take note of the cares and concerns of those I have to share this world with. St Augustine was asked what Christianity is – and he answered, "Humilitas, humilitas, humilitas." The greatest example of this is Jesus himself who "emptied himself and took on the form of a servant" (Philippians 2 v 9).

My old gentleman friend had to admit that he knew more than he thought about Micah. One more point – the name Micah – MIKAYEHU means "who is like God". This is both Micah's name and message. There is none like God and it's only when we know this that we can take his message fully to heart. We do not remember Jesus because he was born in Bethlehem but we remember him because he showed us what it is like truly to:

DO JUSTICE – LOVE MERCY – WALK HUMBLY BEFORE GOD

MATTHEW 5: 1-16

1. Seeing the crowds, he went up on the mountain, and when he sat down his disciples came to him.

2. And he opened his mouth and taught them, saying:

3. "Blessed are the poor in spirit, for theirs is the kingdom of heaven.

4. "Blessed are those who mourn, for they shall be comforted.

5. "Blessed are the meek, for they shall inherit the earth.

6. "Blessed are those who hunger and thirst for righteousness, for they shall be satisfied.

7. "Blessed are the merciful, for they shall obtain mercy.

8. "Blessed are the pure in heart, for they shall see God.

9. "Blessed are the peacemakers, for they shall be called sons of God.

10. "Blessed are those who are persecuted for righteousness' sake, for theirs is the kingdom of heaven.

11. "Blessed are you when men revile you and persecute you and utter all kinds of evil against you falsely on my account.

12. Rejoice and be glad, for your reward is great in heaven, for so men persecuted the prophets who were before you.

13. "You are the salt of the earth; but if salt has lost its taste, how shall its saltness be restored? It is no longer good for anything except to be thrown out and trodden under foot by men.

14. "You are the light of the world. A city set on a hill cannot be hid.

15. Nor do men light a lamp and put it under a bushel, but on a stand, and it gives light to all in the house.

16. Let your light so shine before men, that they may see your good works and give glory to your Father who is in heaven.

4.

"Blessed are the poor in spirit, theirs is the Kingdom of Heaven."

In the Gospels we find that a good deal of Jesus' teaching comes in the form of answers to questions. Perhaps the most famous one is the good Samaritan. Jesus is asked, "What shall I do to inherit eternal life?" Jesus replied by asking his questioner what he had read. He got the reply, "Love the Lord your God with all your heart and mind and soul, and your neighbour as yourself." Jesus told him he answered well – and should put it into practice. But, he was asked the further question, "Who is my neighbour?" (Luke 10).

Jesus had the facility of a story teller and could produce an answer that was both an illuminating answer and at the same time memorable. However, we should note that there is one special part of Jesus' teaching that is not the result of questioning but is the kernel of his teaching out of which all the later answers to questions came, and that is the beatitudes and their explanation (Matthew 5). So, we note the importance of the beatitudes to Jesus because this is what he wanted to say. And more than anything else, we should look at what he puts first – "Blessed are the poor in spirit for theirs is the Kingdom of Heaven." All the other beatitudes arise from this and help us to understand it.

Before we go further, let's just digress for a minute and see what Jesus actually said. Jesus spoke in Aramaic – but the Gospels are written in Greek and the Bibles we have are written in English. So when we read this passage, we are reading at third hand! I do not know what version of the Bible you read at home – there are at least ten versions in English. By all means use a modern version but do not forget the King James, the Authorised Version. In that version, the beatitudes have the word 'are' printed in italics. This is done because the original version from which the translation comes has no verb. To be as accurate as possible, that is, to translate without a verb, we would have to write something like "Oh the bliss of those who are poor in spirit." It's 'exclamation mark' language and reads stronger than "blessed are".

We turn now to ask what Jesus meant by this. "Poor in spirit" sounds kind of negative but we know that coming from Jesus, it won't be negative. We can perhaps approach this by a story.

A Van Gogh painting was reportedly bought by a Japanese billionaire for 75 million dollars. He then, for security, placed it in a vault where it lay unseen for years. This is a kind of parable of our human situation. We find ourselves seeking to give meaning to the life we are living and often we think that one way or another we can find this meaning in possessions. We measure each other by what we have – "he has a Jaguar" – "he gets his suits in Savile Row"

– "she has private health insurance" and so on about designer labels. We attribute to these things an importance which is barely skin deep.

Go back to our Japanese wealthy man – it turns out that there is a question about the authenticity of his Van Gogh. It appears that it is a forgery painted by his doctor! What a discovery – my prized possession that was too valuable to show turns out to have very little value after all! This is Jesus' teaching – we prize the wrong things. And the corollary is that we are blessed if we avoid this emptiness. To be poor in spirit is to have overcome this temptation – to seek to fill our lives with things and thus give them value – it is to see how insignificant we are if we take our meaning from our possessions. So perhaps we should translate this in a more pointed way: "Oh the bliss of those of poor spirit – they are not always wanting!" And when you think about it this should not be very hard. Space is so vast and our place in it so tiny; we should be seeing ourselves in this context, and the Jaguar and designer label hardly increases our significance. It's like an extra speck of dust on the mantelpiece. And when we think of the shortness of our life compared with the age of our planet we truly are little more than a flash of lightning. The poor in spirit recognise this and actually rejoice in it because it removes from them all efforts to give ourselves meaning by transient things.

There's a further point, by recognising the folly of trying to show our importance by acquisition, but instead find our true value by realising that it is God who gives meaning to ourselves. This means that we can learn how to see ourselves as God's creation. This is our true worth. It's no longer something that rusts or breaks down, but it is eternal. With this in mind we can quote how Professor Barclay translated this.

"O the bliss of the man who has realised his own utter helplessness, and who has put his whole trust in God, for this alone can he render to God that perfect obedience which will make him a citizen of the Kingdom of Heaven."

We should notice one more thing; Jesus speaks this in the present tense – "theirs IS the Kingdom of Heaven." This is no future promise of what we might be if we behave ourselves. It is attainable now if we are willing to practise being poor in spirit. "O the bliss" and let us also note that the bliss is far reaching.

William Burns was one of the earliest missionaries to China. He died there and his Chinese followers and friends opened the box that contained his belongings – to find he had nothing of value, only a few personal trinkets. One of his friends seeing this, commented, "He must have been very poor, but he made many rich." That is the product of being poor in spirit. "O the bliss!"

LUKE 10: 29-37

29. But he, desiring to justify himself, said to Jesus, "And who is my neighbor?"

30. Jesus replied, "A man was going down from Jerusalem to Jericho, and he fell among robbers, who stripped him and beat him, and departed, leaving him half dead.

31. Now by chance a priest was going down that road; and when he saw him he passed by on the other side.

32. So likewise a Levite, when he came to the place and saw him, passed by on the other side.

33. But a Samaritan, as he journeyed, came to where he was; and when he saw him, he had compassion,

34. and went to him and bound up his wounds, pouring on oil and wine; then he set him on his own beast and brought him to an inn, and took care of him.

35. And the next day he took out two denarii and gave them to the innkeeper, saying, 'Take care of him; and whatever more you spend, I will repay you when I come back.'

36. Which of these three, do you think, proved neighbour to the man who fell among the robbers?"

37. He said, "The one who showed mercy on him." And Jesus said to him, "Go and do likewise."

5.

"But a Samaritan had compassion."

We all know very well the story of the good Samaritan, and even some people who do not know the story still use the phrase as a description of someone who does a good deed. Yet, although we say we know the story there is a depth in it that sometimes passes us by. Some years ago I had a duty to mark some of the school essays on behalf of the National Bible Society of Scotland – usually the first-year secondary pupils. There was a fairly common way of setting the topic for an essay: "tell in your own words". And as often as not, it was a parable that was chosen. And all these years later I still remember one quite vividly. It was, "Tell in your own words the story of the good Samaritan." And this was the one I remember.

"There was this man who was going along Copland Road on a Saturday afternoon wearing a green and white scarf. (Now for those who don't know, Copland Road is in Glasgow and leads to Ibrox Stadium which is the football park of Glasgow Rangers. Rangers play in blue colours. The man with the green and white scarf was a follower of Celtic – and Celtic and Rangers are fierce opponents – and their supporters tend to be Catholics for Celtic, and Rangers followers are Protestant. So what we have here is a Celtic supporter going to Ibrox to see his side play their foremost opponents. The man in the green and white scarf represents something of this rivalry). He is going along Copland Road when a gang of youths wearing blue and white scarves stop him and give him a hammering and leave him hurt and penniless, and they even took his match ticket. He was leaning against a wall and bleeding and a priest came along and saw him. Time was getting on so he left him and hurried away – he had a complimentary match ticket and thought he might offend the man who gave him the ticket and never get another one. Then a nun came by – she was one of the Little Sisters of Mercy and she was carrying a collection box. She saw the man was wounded but thought to herself that she couldn't risk stopping to help the man, because the sisters needed the money in the box. So she passed by. Then a fellow with a blue and white scarf came along. He looked at the man who was hurt and phoned for an ambulance. He waited till the ambulance came and asked where they would take the man – and he promised to visit the hospital, which he later did. Then he rushed to the match and had missed the kick-off and the first goal. Jesus said we should all be like him."

I commended this boy for a prize, which was a little pocket Bible with a presentation ticket inside the front cover. I commended him because he obviously wrote with feeling and imagination – who else would think to mention that the theft included the match ticket and even worse (maybe), he missed the first goal! I often wonder if he still has that Bible and ever reads it. Yet I gave him the prize despite the fact that his knowledge of the parable was very superficial. He wrote about the parable as it was taught to him. The fact is that the parables of Jesus repay close study because they are much more than stories about good deeds.

The man in the parable was going from Jerusalem to Jericho when he was hijacked. Now it is a feature in stories from the ancient time right up to today that human life is seen as a journey – and we have that here. But the question is, what kind of journey? Here, going from Jerusalem to Jericho (and Jesus' hearers would know this) is downhill all the way, the implication being that it is not just a physical but a moral descent. This is to a certain extent borne out by the next part of the story "he fell among thieves." From this we draw the conclusion that he was travelling alone. This was just not done. The road from Jerusalem to Jericho was not only downhill but was notorious for hijacks. So, it was the practice that travellers waited at Jerusalem city exits until there was a group big enough to travel together in safety, but this man in the parable went alone! Was he a crooked trader who didn't want to risk others seeing what he did? We don't know – but given his moral lifestyle is on the downward path – well – what do you think?

Then there are those who passed by – the priest and the Levite. These were in different ways servants of the temple. But in order to serve they had to keep ritually clean and dealing with blood could render them unclean. Also, there were more temple officials than needed and you could hold the title of Levite all your life and never be asked to officiate in any way. So, it could be suggested that in this story the Levite was getting a chance to serve – a once in a lifetime thing – and he did not wish to render himself unfit! So, it was left to the Samaritan. The suggestion was twofold. Human need comes before temple ritual! And a hated foreigner may in fact be the one to give the help and set an example of neighbourhood loving!

One last point – Jerusalem was the blessed city of the temple. Jericho was the cursed city – Joshua is recorded (Joshua 6 v 26) as placing a curse on Jericho.

The people who heard Jesus' parable would know all this. So, as well as asking who my neighbour is, they would also know that even the one who is travelling from blessedness to cursedness needs neighbourly help. There's a bit more to this parable than match tickets and goals! And all Jesus' stories are like that. He wants us to know the way of righteousness and tells us to beware of the downward route. We're not meant just to look at the superficial, but learn to look with Jesus at the deep truths for life.

JUDGES 6: 11-18

11. Now the angel of the Lord came and sat under the oak at Ophrah, which belonged to Jo'ash the Abiez'rite, as his son Gideon was beating out wheat in the wine press, to hide it from the Mid'ianites.

12. And the angel of the Lord appeared to him and said to him, "The Lord is with you, you mighty man of valor."

13. And Gideon said to him, "Pray, sir, if the Lord is with us, why then has all this befallen us? And where are all his wonderful deeds which our fathers recounted to us, saying, 'Did not the Lord bring us up from Egypt?' But now the Lord has cast us off, and given us into the hand of Mid'ian."

14. And the Lord turned to him and said, "Go in this might of yours and deliver Israel from the hand of Mid'ian; do not I send you?"

15. And he said to him, "Pray, Lord, how can I deliver Israel? Behold, my clan is the weakest in Manas'seh, and I am the least in my family."

16. And the Lord said to him, "But I will be with you, and you shall smite the Mid'ianites as one man."

17. And he said to him, "If now I have found favor with thee, then show me a sign that it is thou who speakest with me.

18. Do not depart from here, I pray thee, until I come to thee, and bring out my present, and set it before thee." And he said, "I will stay till you return."

6.

"But I will be with you."

We all, I am sure, know the work of the Gideons Society. Mainly they place Bibles in hotel rooms. A modern hotel room – specialising in sameness and anonymity – the TV, the low backed chair – the drinks hostess and the Bible. On the odd occasion that I've stayed in such a hotel I've tried to imagine the harassed traveller – away from home for a week – sorting his papers, faxing his orders, phoning home where he wishes he was, then his lonely rest. TV? Piped video? Drinks hostess? Bible? I've noticed that at the introduction to the Bible they now have a list of passages of suggested readings – for the weary – the tempted – the depressed – the anxious, and so on. Now here's a thought for you. If you were asked to give guidance to such a traveller where he should read – what would you recommend? Psalm 23, 'the Lord's my shepherd'; I Corinthians 13, 'there remains these three – faith, hope, love – but the greatest of these is love'; or the Beatitudes 'blessed are they who hunger and thirst after righteousness, for they shall be filled'. Or indeed, the story of Gideon himself?

The Gideon story could be a good one for anyone feeling a bit dejected – kind of fighting a losing battle.

The tribes of Israel were being harassed by neighbours. The routine of life was upset. Take the example of what Gideon was doing – he was threshing grain in the wine press. An early wine press was a hollow in a rock: a threshing floor was big enough to drive a horse through pulling wide rake-like tools – so it was an open ground. So we see that for fear of the neighbouring Midianites, Gideon was having to do it furtively, almost hiding – what would normally be done in the open. He was doing by hand what should be done by horses. Then, we are told, there came a messenger. The word used for messenger is the same as the word for angel. Gideon was very impressed. He knew the great deeds of the past but his present situation was so humiliating that he couldn't see the relevance to him – if the Lord is truly with us then why are we in such a situation? But the 'messenger' (angel) says – why don't you do something about it? Then follows the very human reaction – excuses: self-doubt: why me! I come from the smallest tribe – I'm the youngest in the family. The messenger (angel) meets all these hesitations with the simple statement: "But I will be with you." This marks the breakthrough, the turning point. Up to now we've talked of how God was in the past. Now it's present and personal. "But I will be with you." From now on everything is different. This is the point of the following stories. For example, the offering of food for hospitality becomes a burnt offering, i.e. something done for God – the passage is a bit puzzling to us but it is actually quite simple – it's just a convoluted way of saying "if God is with us ordinary actions have a new significance."

Contemporaries of Gideon would see the message

– with God present there is no such thing as ordinariness and the impossible becomes doable. What follows is derring-do stuff – almost adventure comic material – exaggeration to make the point. If you have the faith to accept what is being promised then the difficult is doable and the impossible is relatively easy and normal! Start with "I will be with you" and go from there and the story is very different. It is to be hoped that the hotel guest takes this to himself.

If we care to go further and then suggest that he opens the Bible at St Matthew's Gospel Chapter 22, he will find Jesus teaching about the Kingdom of God. It's like a king giving a wedding feast for his son. That doesn't need elaboration – it's joyful – nothing is spared – everyone is involved. Now, the Kingdom of Heaven in Jesus' teaching is nothing other than living with the promise: "But I am with you." The Kingdom of Heaven is when ordinariness is turned into godliness – when there's a spring in your step to do your chores because it's a work of service. However, what we find in Jesus' teaching is how many seem unwilling to live in this way. We also find Jesus had a sense of humour. There would be many a smile at his telling of this story.

Let us look at the background to the story. A wedding feast took a bit of organising: usually two invitations were sent out – there was an early invitation – simply, you are invited – but no date or time was given. Then at a later date there was the specific invitation giving date and time – "we're ready now." Some made light of this, choosing to go to the plough or the milking. Fancy having a chance of going to the king's son's wedding and choosing to work in the field instead! Sometimes too, in the case of a rich person – along with the first invitation would be sent appropriate wedding garments so that poorer people would not have the expense of making themselves dress as suitably for such an event. So Jesus is saying – these guests would be, as it were, arriving in the working clothes and leaving the wedding garments at home. This would cause the laughter – but the laughter might falter when the realisation dawns on the hearer: "Here, it's me he's talking about." – "God's promise is to me but I'm too busy to listen." Or of the wedding garments – "Here, look at all the gifts God gives me and I've not used them – or I've used them the wrong way. I'm the one who is missing out on the Kingdom of Heaven." Jesus in this story is by no means demeaning our daily labour but is asking us to laugh at ourselves for getting our priorities wrong.

"But, I will be with you." Our imaginary traveller in his hotel room can meet this promise and Jesus' teaching with humour about the steps we take to live without the promise. Then he has to brave the foggy, crowded motorway the next day and struggle to meet his targets. The big hard world intrudes. I wonder if he'll be like Gideon and live in the promise or like those in Jesus' parable who make light of it. And us? Will we be like the folk who listened to Jesus and laughed until they realised it was themselves he meant. BUT I WILL BE WITH YOU – that's the promise: and it's meant for us too.

PSALM 37: 1-28

1. Fret not yourself because of the wicked, be not envious of wrongdoers!

2. For they will soon fade like the grass, and wither like the green herb.

3. Trust in the Lord, and do good; so you will dwell in the land, and enjoy security.

4. Take delight in the Lord, and he will give you the desires of your heart.

5. Commit your way to the Lord; trust in him, and he will act.

6. He will bring forth your vindication as the light, and your right as the noonday.

7. Be still before the Lord, and wait patiently for him; fret not yourself over him who prospers in his way, over the man who carries out evil devices!

8. Refrain from anger, and forsake wrath! Fret not yourself; it tends only to evil.

9. For the wicked shall be cut off; but those who wait for the Lord shall possess the land.

10. Yet a little while, and the wicked will be no more; though you look well at his place, he will not be there.

11. But the meek shall possess the land, and delight themselves in abundant prosperity.

12. The wicked plots against the righteous, and gnashes his teeth at him;

13. But the Lord laughs at the wicked, for he sees that his day is coming.

14. The wicked draw the sword and bend their bows, to bring down the poor and needy, to slay those who walk uprightly;

15. Their sword shall enter their own heart, and their bows shall be broken.

16. Better is a little that the righteous has than the abundance of many wicked.

17. For the arms of the wicked shall be broken; but the Lord upholds the righteous.

18. The Lord knows the days of the blameless, and their heritage will abide for ever;

19. They are not put to shame in evil times, in the days of famine they have abundance.

20. But the wicked perish; the enemies of the Lord are like the glory of the pastures, they vanish—like smoke they vanish away.

21. The wicked borrows, and cannot pay back, but the righteous is generous and gives;

22. For those blessed by the Lord shall possess the land, but those cursed by him shall be cut off.

23. The steps of a man are from the Lord, and he establishes him in whose way he delights;

24. Though he fall, he shall not be cast headlong, for the Lord is the stay of his hand.

25. I have been young, and now am old; yet I have not seen the righteous forsaken or his children begging bread.

26. He is ever giving liberally and lending, and his children become a blessing.

27. Depart from evil, and do good; so shall you abide for ever.

28. For the Lord loves justice; he will not forsake his saints. The righteous shall be preserved for ever, but the children of the wicked shall be cut off.

7.

"Commit your way to the Lord, trust in Him and He will act."

Having preached a sermon on the work of the Gideon Society, I asked the congregation if they had any suggestions as to where they would like to leave the Bible open in a hotel room for the guests' attention and, hopefully, inspiration. One lady member kindly answered and suggested Psalm 37. What an excellent suggestion it is. It's on the long side but well worth the perseverance. Look at it. Verse 1: "Fret not yourself." Literally translated that reads as: "Don't get all het up!" In the bustle of commercial life when too often everything has to be done by yesterday, it's good to be reminded that we have to manage our pressures. We hear today much about stress and stress-related illnesses.

Verse 3 of the Psalm: "Trust in the Lord, and do good, so you will dwell in the land and enjoy security." This is simple – it means learn to take your creator seriously. He alone knows what he wants of you and trusting in him is liberating – it takes the heat off. There's an old theological formula: "sub speciae aeternitatus" – literally: "from the point of view of eternity." Trusting in the Lord means this – learning to see our life in an eternal framework. How often carrying out this exercise puts our urgency in a different context.

Verse 5 is: "commit yourself to the Lord, and wait patiently for him, and he will act." This is reported to be David Livingstone's favourite verse in Scripture. Often in malarial illness, he not only quoted this but lived it; and time and time again proved it. God will act if you commit to Him.

We could go on like this right through the psalm and undoubtedly learn a lot. But I think we can see the message better if we put it into context. Some time ago I was told a story about a primary school head teacher here in Scotland. School had restarted after the summer holidays and at their first assembly he told them of an experience during his caravan holiday. There was a family in an adjacent caravan who lost their new puppy dog. They spent days searching and asking people if they had seen the dog but with no luck. Finally they agreed, they should have a picnic before the holiday was over. So, they went away for the day and when they returned can you guess what they found at the door of the caravan?

Every hand went up and there was a uniform shout. "The puppy!"

The head teacher shook his head and said, "No, two pints of milk that they had ordered from the caravan office before their outing!"

Great disappointment was felt all round and even a few tears. When he was asked to justify such a story he explained that not everything in life ends the way we would like it to and it was important that children should learn that. Of course, he had a point. A serious and valuable study of children's literature, *The Promise of Happiness* by Fred Inglis examines comics and stories long and short and he dwelt on the phrase "and they all lived happily ever after." He points out that for many children that would just not be the case and he suggested that there should be more of an effort to produce literature that would "fit" children for life, for their real situation and not just always the happy ending.

Both men are right – this is a world of lost puppy dogs and other unpleasant experiences. None of us can escape this. And this is the world that God has made – a world which has sadness as well as happiness – failure as well as success – and we are foolish if we try to pretend it is not like this. But, I believe it's like this for a reason. I never cease to be impressed by people saying to me after a crisis in their life that it was "a growing point; a learning experience." They tell me they discovered depths in themselves they did not know they had. And many of them express it in the terms of the Psalm – they committed themselves to God and discovered he really does act to support and strengthen. In other words, we do not try to ignore or deny the bad times but we show them not as negative only, but as opportunities to open us out to God, and, hopefully make us better people.

There was a BBC newsreader who made it known that he thought it was not right that the news should always end with a good news story – no matter how puerile – Mrs Smith successfully giving her goldfish the kiss of life – designed, as it were, to take our minds off the latest murder or the gruesome details of the current warfare. Good news is there and to be reported but not trivialised – it's people overcoming disability and defeating prejudice, standing up for a principle, etc. That is every bit as important as the bad news!

And that brings us back to where we started. Don't fret, don't get overheated. The psalmist can hardly be understood as being a cock-eyed optimist. He fully knows about the world of lost pups – but he has the message that support is there – trust in God, let Him act. He knows there is much wickedness in the world but he knows that to concentrate on that is to give it a victory; in almost every verse he tells us not to surrender – but learn to trust. St Paul makes the distinction between legal and edifying. It's not illegal to tell infants the story of a lost pup. But it is not edifying! It doesn't build them up. And for edifying St Paul always means to lead them to Jesus. What we are to see is not a sinful wicked humanity, but a humanity capable of growth through crisis, a humanity capable of redemption. Don't get het up about the wicked and bad things – let Jesus help you to grow through them. Wickedness comes and goes in different ways but Jesus' redemption is always there and always the same – positive.

One last point, Psalm 37 in its original Hebrew is what is known as an acrostic – it was written in a way that helped the reader to remember it. A common acrostic for example was to begin every verse with the next letter of the alphabet. We do not have Psalm 37 in such a format in the English language – but it's not particularly difficult to remember. Don't fret – don't get het up – trust the Lord – commit to Him and He will act. Not only is it not difficult – but it's well worth it.

JOHN 2: 1-12

1. On the third day there was a marriage at Cana in Galilee, and the mother of Jesus was there;

2. Jesus also was invited to the marriage, with his disciples.

3. When the wine gave out, the mother of Jesus said to him, "They have no wine."

4. And Jesus said to her, "O woman, what have you to do with me? My hour has not yet come."

5. His mother said to the servants, "Do whatever he tells you."

6. Now six stone jars were standing there, for the Jewish rites of purification, each holding twenty or thirty gallons.

7. Jesus said to them, "Fill the jars with water." And they filled them up to the brim.

8. He said to them, "Now draw some out, and take it to the steward of the feast." So they took it.

9. When the steward of the feast tasted the water now become wine, and did not know where it came from (though the servants who had drawn the water knew), the steward of the feast called the bridegroom

10. And said to him, "Every man serves the good wine first; and when men have drunk freely, then the poor wine; but you have kept the good wine until now."

11. This, the first of his signs, Jesus did at Cana in Galilee, and manifested his glory; and his disciples believed in him.

12. After this he went down to Caper'na-um, with his mother and his brothers and his disciples; and there they stayed for a few days.

8.
"Do Whatever He Tells You."

The former Professor of New Testament at Manchester University, T W Manson, writing about the Gospels said "reading St John is a different experience from the other Gospels, so much so that we can say "fools and bairns should not see things half done." And here in Chapter 2 we have an example of why he said this. We have here the tension between the good news of Jesus and his unfavourable judgement on human conduct motivated by greed and unfairness. The clarity of the distinction between life lived by Gospel values and life without them could not be clearer.

We start by looking at the story of the wine shortage at the wedding feast. This story only occurs in John's Gospel and, needless to say is not the favourite story of the temperance lobby. But, if we try to see the story as it would be seen by Jesus' contemporaries I think we can see it in a different light. Let me put it this way: the Romans and the Greeks had gods who were associated with wine – Bacchus and Dionysus. Indeed we have in our vocabulary the term 'bacchanalia' which has come to mean a drunken party. And there is also the Old

Testament acknowledgement that among God's gifts is "wine to gladden the heart of man" (Psalm 104). What we are told in this story is that Jesus can do anything Dionysus or Bacchus can, but better! "But you have kept the best wine until last!" And the people of the day, who were not as literal as we are, would know the meaning of the story.

I suggest that we try to view this passage as the contemporeria did. Put it this way: if Mr Abrahams was down in Cana at the time of this wedding he would tell his wife on returning home that Jesus was being talked of in terms of John's story. His wife would not ask, "Was it sauvignon blanc or chardonnay?" She would know at once that a claim was being made about Jesus – that his teaching was superior to the other gods. An old minister friend of mine had the expression "if religion is the wine of life, then Jesus' wine was champagne."

The next picture St John gives us of Jesus is very different. We move from the Jesus of celebration to the Jesus of anger. The background to this story of the cleansing of the temple is one of cheating and corruption. Israel has the geographical location which made it a passageway between the countries of the north and south of the Mediterranean Sea. Unlike today, there were no phones or international banking arrangements. So, the idea of an agreed exchange rate between different countries was not to be found. This did not matter too much to regular travellers such as army personnel, they were experienced enough to avoid being overcharged. But, Jerusalem was also a place of pilgrimage for the Jewish nation. Jewish pilgrims from far and wide came to the temple and, if they could afford it, they presented a sacrifice – a dove or a lamb – depending on financial circumstances. Further, the temple expected pilgrims to make their financial contributions in Shekels only. The upshot was that the temple money changers regularly overcharged pilgrims – particularly those they deemed gullible. Also, the stalls on the temple precinct sold animals for sacrifice expensively. The same animals could be bought in the town considerably cheaper. However, there was in the temple area an inspectorate to see that the sacrifice offerings were in perfect condition – suitable to be offered to God. And, surprise, surprise, the animals bought in the town failed the inspection regularly, whereas those bought in the temple grounds always passed. Needless to say, there was an "arrangement" between the inspectors and the stallholders and the losers were the poor pilgrims. Jesus could see it was always the innocent pilgrims who were the losers. Accordingly, Jesus showed his anger against those who exploited the pilgrims. This story occurs in the other Gospels but at the end of Jesus' life. In St John it comes right at the beginning and is in contrast to the Jesus of the wedding feast. By so arranging these stories St John is making it clear to us that our experience of Jesus can be either of celebration or arousing his wrath. And in these stories we're given the hint on what matters, vis, the words of his mother – she tells the stewards of the wedding, "Do whatever he tells you."

This too is the message for all of us. The Jesus we meet depends on how we live. If we live trying to "do what he tells you" – we meet the Jesus of love and celebration. But if we let greed and exploiting determine our way of living – then we meet his wrath.

It's up to us. Which Jesus do we prefer?

Jesus' agenda for the world is that we should learn to celebrate God's goodness and love – and we have been given the freedom to make this our agenda too.

LUKE 18: 9-17

9. He also told this parable to some who trusted in themselves that they were righteous and despised others:

10. "Two men went up into the temple to pray, one a Pharisee and the other a tax collector.

11. The Pharisee stood and prayed thus with himself, 'God, I thank thee that I am not like other men, extortioners, unjust, adulterers, or even like this tax collector.

12. I fast twice a week, I give tithes of all that I get.'

13. But the tax collector, standing far off, would not even lift up his eyes to heaven, but beat his breast, saying, 'God, be merciful to me a sinner!'

14. I tell you, this man went down to his house justified rather than the other; for every one who exalts himself will be humbled, but he who humbles himself will be exalted."

15. Now they were bringing even infants to him that he might touch them; and when the disciples saw it, they rebuked them.

16. But Jesus called them to him, saying, "Let the children come to me, and do not hinder them; for to such belongs the kingdom of God.

17. Truly, I say to you, whoever does not receive the kingdom of God like a child shall not enter it."

9.

"Everyone who exalts himself will be humbled but he who humbles himself will be exalted."

The late Professor William Barclay liked to tell a story of a journey by train to England from Glasgow to fulfil a preaching engagement. As he was passing through the Yorkshire moors he glanced out of the window and saw a small house, painted white which stood out almost sparkling against the countryside. A couple of days later on his journey home he looked to see the house again. But in the interim it had snowed and the white house appeared dingy and almost dirty against nature's whiteness that now surrounded it. And of course, the obvious point is, how do we make our comparisons? Sometimes it is very difficult.

Rabbi Lionel Blue tells the story of a funeral he had to take of a man he described as simply a rogue. He hunted for something to say at the funeral and after much thinking he said that the best he could was, "Compared to his brother he was a saint!" If we compare ourselves to the Hitlers and Saddam Husseins we can convince ourselves of our saintliness also. We can list the people we would like to be compared with and come away with the thought, *Well at least I'm not as bad as Jimmy Saville*, or, *I am more honest than Robert Maxwell*. And if we are satisfied with "at least I'm not whatever" we fool ourselves into thinking everything is all right.

This is a theme that is present in religious teaching from the earliest times. Physical strength, fighting cunning, long life and many other human attributes can be interpreted as in some way a sign of godliness. A good example of this is Samson in the book of Judges. If he behaved publicly as we read in the Bible in modern times he would give the tabloid newspapers a field day. In many ways, the Old Testament standards of godliness were fairly permissive. It was John Calvin, the reformer, in many ways the founder of the Church to which we belong, who described the crudity of many of our human comparisons in terms of our eyesight. He suggested we should think what it is like to look at the ground and see in detail what is there, and then marvel at how good our eyesight is. But then we should look at the sun and find our eyes are dazzled. Calvin draws the conclusion that true wisdom consists of two parts: knowledge of God and knowledge of ourselves. And he further concluded that we cannot have true knowledge of ourselves without first being dazzled by the knowledge of God.

This, in a most graphic way, is what Jesus is teaching us in this parable in Luke 18 from which we take the text: "Everyone who exalts himself will be humbled but he who humbles himself will be exalted." There is a lot in it that needs a bit of explanation.

The religious obligations referred to here are intended for all Jews: fasting and tithing. The requirement was that there should be one fast in the year and that one tenth of the earnings from agricultural pursuits should be given over to the temple. But our Pharisee here is boasting that he is especially righteous – he fasted, not once a year, but twice a week, and he didn't tithe only his agricultural income but all his income from all sources. In other words he was saying – "Look at me, how good I am." Now notice how Jesus tells the story – the word he puts into the Pharisee's mouth most often is "I" – I give more, I fast more, I am not like other people, extortioners, unjust, adulterers – or even like this tax collector standing here. I imagine our reaction would be: what a sanctimonious big-head. He might have performed more religious duties than the requirement, but he had not conquered the sin of pride – and his comparison of himself with the tax collector is rude in the extreme. Certainly not someone we would wish as a friend. And it is reasonable to conclude that Jesus thought such behaviour was less than desirable. And when we turn to the tax collector there is a translation point that we should note. Both the Authorised and Revised Standard translations present us with "Lord have mercy on me, a sinner" – whereas the correct translation actually is – "Lord have mercy on me THE sinner." In other words, there was nobody he could compare himself with. In God's presence he was so dazzled by the perfection he met that he saw he had nothing to boast of. In the field of self-understanding he was miles away from the Pharisee. And Jesus asks us the question in his parable implicitly – who had the better understanding of God? And he gives us his answer "the tax collector went down to his house justified rather than the Pharisee – for everyone who exalts himself will be humbled, but he who humbles himself will be exalted."

Jesus' point is very simple. Faith is not a series of actions we perform, however good, but, what matters more is our relationship to God. And that relationship, properly understood is always one of humility.

Robert Burns in his satirical poem "To a Louse" has the verse:

"O wad some power the giftie gie us
To see oursels as others see us
It wad frae mony a blunder free us
and foolish notion."

Jesus gives us that power if only we will heed him.

EPHESIANS 1: 3-14

3. Blessed be the God and Father of our Lord Jesus Christ, who has blessed us in Christ with every spiritual blessing in the heavenly places,

4. Even as he chose us in him before the foundation of the world, that we should be holy and blameless before him.

5. He destined us in love to be his sons through Jesus Christ, according to the purpose of his will,

6. To the praise of his glorious grace which he freely bestowed on us in the Beloved.

7. In him we have redemption through his blood, the forgiveness of our trespasses, according to the riches of his grace

8. Which he lavished upon us.

9. For he has made known to us in all wisdom and insight the mystery of his will, according to his purpose which he set forth in Christ

10. As a plan for the fullness of time, to unite all things in him, things in heaven and things on earth.

11. In him, according to the purpose of him who accomplishes all things according to the counsel of his will,

12. We who first hoped in Christ have been destined and appointed to live for the praise of his glory.

13. In him you also, who have heard the word of truth, the gospel of your salvation, and have believed in him, were sealed with the promised Holy Spirit,

14. Which is the guarantee of our inheritance until we acquire possession of it, to the praise of his glory.

10.

"For he has made known to us in all wisdom and insight the mystery of his will according to his purpose which he set forth in Christ."

From time to time I have been asked, as most ministers have, to verify that a photograph is a true likeness of the person who wants such a photograph for a passport or a driving licence. In so doing I have to state that I am a recognised person whose verification can be relied upon – in any case the designation is "minister of religion." (I also have to say that on occasion I felt that I was in some way perjuring myself – as the photograph was not really a true likeness, even sometimes looking less than human!) But that aside, I feel uncomfortable at having to write "minister of religion". Religion is an ambiguous word. There are many people who equate "religion" with violence and superstition. Just think about Northern Ireland. Catholics and Protestants seem to practise a religion of prejudice and hatred. We think of Islam which rewards warfare and killing with the promise of a glorious life hereafter. And think of the poor untouchables in India. We could go on and on and it's not a nice story. It was John Wesley, the founder of the Methodist Church, who said of some of his opponents who belonged to another branch of the Christian Church – "Your God is my Devil." And this is not just historical – superstition and violence are as alive today as at any time in history. Frankly I do not mean any of these things when I sign a passport photograph.

To try to reach an understanding of "religion" I turn to St Paul and his vision of "a plan for the fullness of time made known in Jesus." Here is an affirmation that could not be clearer. God has a plan that he is working to. The word translated as "plan" is "oikonomia" which as well as being translated as "plan" can equally be translated as "economy" or even "management". "God is managing our world" is what Paul is telling us. This is no vague woolly faith – the kind that says, "I suppose there must be a God." No. This is a deep conviction that God is a hands-on God – involved in his creation – and managing it. This is not always an easy thing to believe – indeed sometimes it's almost easier to believe that the world is mismanaged – when you see the African baby trying to suckle at its mother's shrivelled and milkless breast – when you read of the inhumanity of man to man in Auschwitz or the killing fields of Cambodia. How can God be in charge when such things are allowed to happen? Indeed, I know of many people who have given up on faith because there is just so much suffering in the world. But Paul was not unaware of the suffering and injustice and cruelty. Paul himself in his time was both persecutor and persecuted. He looked on at the execution of Stephen (Acts 6 and 7) and we are told "Saul was consenting to his death." Also we remember that Paul was eventually executed himself and had a good time of his life imprisoned. But still he could say, "God has a plan." He could say this because of Jesus.

We ask ourselves the question – how else do you explain Jesus? Either he was an immature altruist with a martyr complex and as such an interesting subject for research for psychiatrists and a footnote in a textbook on mental health. Or, and what a pregnant word that 'or' is, or Jesus is what the Gospel of John tells us he is: "the way, the truth and the life." For Paul this was the case – Jesus and Jesus alone made sense of the world. Only in his is there any ultimate hope in the word. Only in him could the true God be seen – not the gods made in our image to support our cultures – the fashion gods whose will and message has no consistency but change according to our needs – the god who made black people to be the slaves of white: who gave his blessing to some but withheld it from others. The true God who manages the world shows us by suffering love where hope is to be found and where our future lies. And having discerned this, Paul pours out the implications. And he expresses it in a forceful way. It is worth noting that Paul declares how he sees true faith – and please note that in the original Greek St Paul goes from Ephesians Chapter 1 verse 3 to verse 14 without stopping for even a comma – it just pours right out of him. BLESSING – FORGIVENESS – GRACE – WISDOM – MYSTERY – REVEALED – UNITY IN CHRIST – this is the content of God's management. That's what Paul saw in Jesus and it made sense of the world because it all meant God loves us. The Scottish comedian Rikki Fulton in his autobiography mentions his churchgoing and his minister preaching "put a spring in your step". God loves us and is on our side in our life's journey if only we will allow him.

What a long way that insight that God loves us is from the religion of violence; hatred of neighbour; superstition; judgementalism. Not everyone that says unto me "Lord, Lord" is fit for the Kingdom of Heaven – this is what happens when we try to make God in our image. But when we share with Paul the insight that God loves us – then we too can enjoy that spring in our step. The famous theologian, Karl Barth, said Christianity is not a religion – it's a Gospel. How much more meaningful that word is "GOSPEL" I only wish I could write that on the passport photos, "minister of the Gospel". Indeed, that is what we are all called to be – not just the person with the backward facing collar – but all the followers of Jesus, by action, by caring and supporting, by praying – we all are ministers because we all witness to Jesus who taught us that God loves us – the Gospel!

ACTS 17: 16-31

16. Now while Paul was waiting for them at Athens, his spirit was provoked within him as he saw that the city was full of idols.

17. So he argued in the synagogue with the Jews and the devout persons, and in the market place every day with those who chanced to be there.

18. Some also of the Epicurean and Stoic philosophers met him. And some said, "What would this babbler say?" Others said, "He seems to be a preacher of foreign divinities"—because he preached Jesus and the resurrection.

19. And they took hold of him and brought him to the Are-op'agus, saying, "May we know what this new teaching is which you present?

20. For you bring some strange things to our ears; we wish to know therefore what these things mean."

21. Now all the Athenians and the foreigners who lived there spent their time in nothing except telling or hearing something new.

22. So Paul, standing in the middle of the Are-op'agus, said: "Men of Athens, I perceive that in every way you are very religious.

23. For as I passed along, and observed the objects of your worship, I found also an altar with this inscription, 'To an unknown god.' What therefore you worship as unknown, this I proclaim to you.

24. The God who made the world and everything in it, being Lord of heaven and earth, does not live in shrines made by man,

25. Nor is he served by human hands, as though he needed anything, since he himself gives to all men life and breath and everything.

26. And he made from one every nation of men to live on all the face of the earth, having determined allotted periods and the boundaries of their habitation,

27. That they should seek God, in the hope that they might feel after him and find him. Yet he is not far from each one of us,

28. For 'In him we live and move and have our being'; as even some of your poets have said, 'For we are indeed his offspring.'

29. Being then God's offspring, we ought not to think that the Deity is like gold, or silver, or stone, a representation by the art and imagination of man.

30. The times of ignorance God overlooked, but now he commands all men everywhere to repent,

31. Because he has fixed a day on which he will judge the world in righteousness by a man whom he has appointed, and of this he has given assurance to all men by raising him from the dead."

11.

"He noticed how full of idols the city was."

Some years before St Paul visited Athens there had been a serious pestilence and much loss of life – we are not sure what the disease was but there were many deaths. There seemed to be no remedy and one city leader suggested that they should take a flock of sheep and set them free. They should then watch them and wherever they lay down to sleep they should be killed as a sacrifice to the nearest god, and hopefully appease the god who sent the plague. Of course, some sheep took their rest near no shrine, so these were sacrificed to an unknown god. The result was that in Athens there were a number of shrines to an unknown god. The notion of an unknown god is an interesting comment on human understanding and search for truth. No matter how many ways humans see God there is always room for more. No matter how many gods there are, there is always room for another. The truth that underlines this thinking is that the Athenians think that God or the gods are greater than the human capacity to understand. And the fact that this was in Athens very much makes this observation all the more interesting. Athens in the ancient world was the city of human learning and scholarship – the home of Socrates, Plato, and Aristotle – and even here no one claimed to understand God. In Paul's day it was philosophical schools and their theories he was faced with. The Epicurians believed that God was so remote that he was unknowable. On the other hand, the Stoics believed the gods were so near that they were in fact the cause of everything and you just had to accept that. Paul was dealing with two extremes of thinking.

St Paul comes into this Athens and we are told "he noticed how full of idols the city was." The Christian faith has been dismissive of idols and has seen them as marks of the pagan and in essence evil. This can be seen today in parts of Africa where medicine men who are also named witch doctors are denounced from pulpits. The result is enmity and entrenchment. St Paul surely had the better attitude – see the idol as the expression of a deeply felt need. And it was to this deep need that he tried to address his message. It is a passage of scripture that has attracted a great deal of attention. New Testament scholars, theologians, philosophers, all have analysed it. It's a passage to come back to time and again. But let us just observe two ways of understanding how Paul responded to the city full of idols.

a) You have shown you do not know it all. I'll try to tell you what you don't know. Now, we have to be very careful here. There is a form of argument called "the God of the gaps." In other words find a gap in human knowledge and fill it with God. Negatively this can mean God is not knowable in human wisdom but only in human ignorance. Also, it can end up with us having a temporary God – that is, a God we can believe in until we learn better! This is not St Paul's way. Instead he said effectively, "I'll show you what Jesus told us about God – I'll tell you how Jesus taught us to see God as HE wants to be seen. In Jesus God revealed Himself – not as a stop-gap – but as a life-giving force called love."

b) Paul was a good Jew. And part of his education would be the story of Moses who was told "no man can see God and live." But Paul knew from his personal experience that in Jesus, God has shown us all we need to know to live a life as he would have us live – that is – showing that we are "made in His image." Put simply Paul is saying – "I'll show you what you need to know because God has shown it to me in the life and love of Jesus." No argument – no looking for a gap in knowledge, but an affirmation of the God of love.

How full of idols the city was. We do not live in the religious society that Athens was. We seek our happiness and lifestyle in different ways. However, we would be wrong to look on the Athenians and see them as superstitious and ignorant of a truly godly way of life. We just need to look at our society to see what we think is the true way to live – we have status symbols, we have drugs, we have sexual conquests. Watch our TV programmes for a day and ask yourself if this is a Christian country any more than Athens. We seek our fulfilment without any reference to God. We need again a St Paul to tell us what we need to know. I heard a story of a primary school head teacher asking a young pupil who Jesus was. She got the answer, apparently – "God with his skin on." We may think that's a bit crude – but it really is just another way of translating the passage in St John's Gospel "and the word became flesh and dwelt among us." God as he is in Himself is not knowable by humans – that would kill their humanity. But, the word made flesh is knowable – and the more we know of him the less we need our lives and our cities to be "full of idols."

MATTHEW 7: 15-29

15. "Beware of false prophets, who come to you in sheep's clothing but inwardly are ravenous wolves.

16. You will know them by their fruits. Are grapes gathered from thorns, or figs from thistles?

17. So, every sound tree bears good fruit, but the bad tree bears evil fruit.

18. A sound tree cannot bear evil fruit, nor can a bad tree bear good fruit.

19. Every tree that does not bear good fruit is cut down and thrown into the fire.

20. Thus you will know them by their fruits.

21. "Not every one who says to me, 'Lord, Lord,' shall enter the kingdom of heaven, but he who does the will of my Father who is in heaven.

22. On that day many will say to me, 'Lord, Lord, did we not prophesy in your name, and cast out demons in your name, and do many mighty works in your name?'

23. And then will I declare to them, 'I never knew you; depart from me, you evildoers.'

24. "Every one then who hears these words of mine and does them will be like a wise man who built his house upon the rock;

25. And the rain fell, and the floods came, and the winds blew and beat upon that house, but it did not fall, because it had been founded on the rock.

26. And every one who hears these words of mine and does not do them will be like a foolish man who built his house upon the sand;

27. And the rain fell, and the floods came, and the winds blew and beat against that house, and it fell; and great was the fall of it."

28. And when Jesus finished these sayings, the crowds were astonished at his teaching,

29. For he taught them as one who had authority, and not as their scribes.

12.

"He taught as one who had Authority, not as the Scribes."

One of the foremost theologians of the twentieth century, Karl Barth, on a visit to Great Britain was asked by a radio interviewer what he would like to be if he wasn't a theologian. He replied, "A traffic policeman because he has real authority – when he holds up his hand we stop, when he beckons with his hand we go, however he signals we obey. We recognise his authority." And, of course, that is true. "Authority" in a simple contained situation is easily defined and is also acceptable – it is in all our interests. On the battlefield in a war situation, knowing who has the authority to organise is vital. In a school classroom the teacher must have authority to carry through the learning situation – a weak teacher is not welcome! Wrongly used authority can lead to chaos. Modern China is a case in point. Mau Tse Tung had the authority to make decisions in virtue of his position and so he introduced the one child per family policy. Now parents of girls try to make them more desirable by spending money – if a boy agrees to marry her, the parents will buy the house, the car, etc. Society is suffering from this misuse of authority. It will take two or three generations to restore a healthy balance.

History is full of instances of the abuse of authority – the slave trade assumed the white man had authority over the black. Parliamentary authority for a long time used its authority to withhold the right to vote from women, it had the legal authority to do so – but as the suffragettes made clear, they did not have the moral authority. Our text today is that Jesus taught with authority, not as the scribes. How are we to understand his use of the word?

Let us look first at the last part of our text: "not as the scribes." The scribes were the educated people – they were serious and generally sincere. But they had been taught how to interpret scriptures and the history of their faith. They were the teachers and interpreters of the law. However, there was a problem – the way they interpreted the law was both open to abuse and often not helpful. For example, take the commandment about working on the Sabbath day – and working for example had to be defined. It was suggested that working included travelling to and from home to your work. So the next question was, what is meant by home? So the definition came up – home is where you cook and eat your food. This was quite easy to get round. If you were well enough off you could build a little shed at appropriate distance from your home where you actually lived – and in this shed you could have the ancient equivalent of a primus stove and a can of baked beans. So your travelling was limitless if you had enough sheds and the fitness to travel between them. In such a way the law lost its purpose. Also, if you asked the scribe for the answer to a problem, you could not rely on getting an answer. What you got was a series of answers – well, "Rabbi A says this and Rabbi B says this and so on." It was the scholarship of ambiguity. Remember Topol in Fiddler on the Roof. In the song "If I Were a Rich Man" he would have the leisure to "Listen to the wise men – that would be the finest gift of all." It was casuistry and confusion – but if you had that kind of mind – I suppose – enjoyable.

Now over and against this, listen to Jesus. "You have heard it said... BUT I say unto you." No references to scribes or wise men but the simplicity – I say it unto you, i.e. you have heard it said you shall not kill – but I say unto you, "DO NOT EVEN BE ANGRY," and you have heard it said you shall not commit adultery, but I say unto you, "DO NOT EVEN LOOK AT A WOMAN WITH LUST IN YOUR EYE." Jesus was able to offer these answers to our problems because he had authority, and an authority that was obvious. Not "home is where you cook and eat your food" but a challenge to think it through – "the Sabbath is made for man and not man for the Sabbath." I.e. not a human idea that invites our ingenuity in inventing interpretations that enable us to negate the meaning, but a call to see ourselves in the light of our Creator.

We are two thousand years on from the time of Jesus and we live in a vastly different world. We are told we live in a "post-modern" generation, although I have to say I don't know what that means. We live in a time when science seeks to prove claims about how we see the world. And very often scientists reject religious claims because they cannot be proved. But if we look at the teaching of Jesus we see that love is stronger than hate and more positive in human affairs – surely time after time we see this to be proven in our relationships if we are brave enough to attempt it. Forgiveness is more positive than retribution. Jesus' authority in these sayings is not just for his own generation but for all human history. And it is an authority we reject to our own impoverishment.

There is a story about a New York lady hostess who held regular "get-together" evenings for interesting and talented people – authors, musicians, poets, and academics. On one particular occasion one of her guests was an elderly priest. One by one the guests displayed their talents and the evening went well. But the priest became aware that he was going to have to take a turn and was somewhat apprehensive – he could not sing or play an instrument and he awaited his turn with some apprehension. And when his turn came he just stood and said quietly, "The Lord is my shepherd; I shall not want. He maketh me to lie down in green pastures; he leadeth me in the paths of righteousness for his name's sake. Yea, through I walk through the valley of the shadow of death, I will fear no evil: for thou art with me, thy rod and thy staff they comfort me. Thou preparest a table before me in the presence of mine enemies, thou annointest my head with oil, my cup runneth over. Surely goodness and mercy shall follow me all the days of my life and I will dwell in the house of the Lord for ever."

As he began to speak there were various conversations going on amongst the guests. But one by one they stopped and there was a very meaningful silence. It was one of those moments when eternity silences our business. And when he finished the silence remained so for a good few moments before all was as before. The hostess standing near a prominent actor asked him, "How would you have done that?" He replied that he would have done it very differently – voice modulations – hand and arm gestures – pauses for effect. But he added – it would not have been as meaningful – "Because, I only know the psalm, he knows the shepherd."

The word used in Matthew's Gospel for authority is the Greek word "Exousia" which means "resources". Jesus had these resources – he knew the Shepherd, in fact we call him the son of God – the Shepherd. And because Jesus lived in unbroken fellowship with the Shepherd he could speak to us in a way that needs our attention for the sake of humanity – it comes from the source of life itself.

2 Kings 5: 1-19 and Luke 17: 11-19

2 KINGS 5: 1-19

1. Na'aman, commander of the army of the king of Syria, was a great man with his master and in high favour, because by him the Lord had given victory to Syria. He was a mighty man of valour, but he was a leper.

2. Now the Syrians on one of their raids had carried off a little maid from the land of Israel, and she waited on Na'aman's wife.

3. She said to her mistress, "Would that my lord were with the prophet who is in Samar'ia! He would cure him of his leprosy."

4. So Na'aman went in and told his lord, "Thus and so spoke the maiden from the land of Israel."

5. And the king of Syria said, "Go now, and I will send a letter to the king of Israel." So he went, taking with him ten talents of silver, six thousand shekels of gold, and ten festal garments.

6. And he brought the letter to the king of Israel, which read, "When this letter reaches you, know that I have sent to you Na'aman my servant, that you may cure him of his leprosy."

7. And when the king of Israel read the letter, he rent his clothes and said, "Am I God, to kill and to make alive, that this man sends word to me to cure a man of his leprosy? Only consider, and see how he is seeking a quarrel with me."

8. But when Eli'sha the man of God heard that the king of Israel had rent his clothes, he sent to the king, saying, "Why have you rent your clothes? Let him come now to me, that he may know that there is a prophet in Israel."

9. So Na'aman came with his horses and chariots, and halted at the door of Eli'sha's house.

10. And Eli'sha sent a messenger to him, saying, "Go and wash in the Jordan seven times, and your flesh shall be restored, and you shall be clean."

11. But Na'aman was angry, and went away, saying, "Behold, I thought that he would surely come out to me, and stand, and call on the name of the Lord his God, and wave his hand over the place, and cure the leper.

12. Are not Aba'na and Pharpar, the rivers of Damascus, better than all the waters of Israel? Could I not wash in them, and be clean?" So he turned and went away in a rage.

13. But his servants came near and said to him, "My father, if the prophet had commanded you to do some great thing, would you not have done it? How much rather, then, when he says to you, 'Wash, and be clean'?"

14. So he went down and dipped himself seven times in the Jordan, according to the word of the man of God; and his flesh was restored like the flesh of a little child, and he was clean.

15. Then he returned to the man of God, he and all his company, and he came and stood before him; and he said, "Behold, I know that there is no God in all the earth but in Israel; so accept now a present from your servant."

16. But he said, "As the Lord lives, whom I serve, I will receive none." And he urged him to take it, but he refused.

17. Then Na'aman said, "If not, I pray you, let there be given to your servant two mules' burden of earth; for henceforth your servant will not offer burnt offering or sacrifice to any god but the Lord.

18. In this matter may the Lord pardon your servant: when my master goes into the house of Rimmon to worship there, leaning on my arm, and I bow myself in the house of Rimmon, when I bow myself in the house of Rimmon, the Lord pardon your servant in this matter."

19. He said to him, "Go in peace."

LUKE 17: 11-19

11. On the way to Jerusalem he was passing along between Samar'ia and Galilee.

12. And as he entered a village, he was met by ten lepers, who stood at a distance

13. And lifted up their voices and said, "Jesus, Master, have mercy on us."

14. When he saw them he said to them, "Go and show yourselves to the priests." And as they went they were cleansed.

15. Then one of them, when he saw that he was healed, turned back, praising God with a loud voice;

16. And he fell on his face at Jesus' feet, giving him thanks. Now he was a Samaritan.

17. Then said Jesus, "Were not ten cleansed? Where are the nine?

18. Was no one found to return and give praise to God except this foreigner?"

19. And he said to him, "Rise and go your way; your faith has made you well."

13.

"He was a man of mighty valour, but he was a leper."

A doctor friend of mine told me of his experience with an elderly male patient. The man attended the surgery because he had acquired a septic foot. The doctor only examined him and gave him a prescription. To his surprise the man turned up at the next day's surgery and suggested to the doctor that he had made a mistake – he presented him with a bottle of pills and suggested the doctor should really have given him an ointment. The doctor realised the patient's ignorance of how his body worked – no knowledge of the circulatory system and the blood's role in carrying a cure to the infected area. So he gave a second prescription for an ointment but handed him back the pills and suggested he should take these as well – just in case they might help. It reminds us that it is only relatively recent in human history that we have gained a reasonably scientific knowledge of our own bodies. It's not that long ago you might have been told to go to bed and tie a dead fish onto the sole of your foot or other such bizarre idea. And amazingly, quite often, the remedies worked! But psychologically there has to be some kind of correlation between the expectation and the treatment.

This was what was lacking in the case of Naaman. We're told that Naaman was a brave warrior, a leader of soldiers, a V.I.P. But he was treated in a manner that seemed to him contemptuous. Elisha didn't even come out of his house to see or speak to him. He just sent a message. "Go and wash in the Jordan seven times and you will be cleaned." Jordan to him was an insignificant stream. Are not Abana and Pharpar, rivers of Damascus, better than all the rivers of Israel? May I not wash in them and be clean? Naaman was ready to have his bravery tested – he would have withstood the force of the flow of these rivers – he would have stood to attention while Elisha called the gods – he would have endured without flinching while Elisha called the gods – he would have flashes or thunder claps or earthquakes if that's what it would take – he was brave enough. But, he was not prepared to be, as he saw it, humiliated. That just did not meet his expectations. Of course, you'll be aware that there is an undercurrent in the story. Whatever the true nature of the encounter between Naaman and Elisha the story as we have it is for public consumption. And the point being made is, of course, that Israel's God is more powerful than the other gods. There was at this time a tendency to think that each country had its own god – hence the later feature in the story when Naaman requests to be allowed to take home some of the soil of Israel – so that he could stand on it and bless the Israel's God! But if we strip the propaganda out of the story, what we learn is that Naaman, despite all his power and bravery, had to learn he should be humble before God. And with persuasion he submitted and was cured. We must not allow the nationalistic contest to blind us – we must, too, see the need to be humble. Of course, God wants to give us, and does give us strengths and gifts which may lead us to considerable achievements – but we must resist glorying in these and remember their source and learn how to use them as God would have us do.

The only immediate similarity between Naaman and the lepers in St Luke's story is that they were cured. Yet, in fact, although in a very different way we meet the same theme. The theme in St Luke is not simple ingratitude – but lack of recognition. In Jesus, God became man – that's what sorts out the Christian faith from all other faiths. But the man did not walk round with a halo or any other features that sorted him out from everyone else in a special way. In fact, the stumbling block to many was, in fact, his ordinariness. And these lepers saw him as just another healer, who this time luckily for them had the appropriate formula. In the despairing nature of their illness they did not look at what was really happening to them – and although healed, they missed the chance of meeting the true God. That's why the proper response was lacking. It's easy for us to sit in judgment with 2,000 years of insight. But it really was very difficult to recognise really who Jesus was. The fact that one of the ten came back adds to this difficulty. That he was a Samaritan – a noted foreigner – raises the question of recognition of Jesus in a new way. Soren Kierkegaard, the Danish theologian, said that many who had lived at the same time as Jesus did not recognise him. But to recognise him in any age was to see him as the moral teacher who was a model of selflessness. But do we really go the next step and take on the enormity of the claim that he is God incarnate? That is true recognition.

Our expectations of God may not always be met by the realities we encounter as we make our way through life. Our prayers may not always be answered as we would hope or expect. Perhaps we have to learn to turn the equation round and expect the unexpected – learn that it is not what we expect of him that really matters but what He expects of us.

One last word. "Your faith has made you well" – not really. Instead, "Your faith has saved you." If it's salvation that we wish and not just another favour, we really do have to practise trying to learn what God expects of us.

GENESIS 9: 8-17

8. Then God said to Noah and to his sons with him,

9. "Behold, I establish my covenant with you and your descendants after you,

10. And with every living creature that is with you, the birds, the cattle, and every beast of the earth with you, as many as came out of the ark

11. I establish my covenant with you, that never again shall all flesh be cut off by the waters of a flood, and never again shall there be a flood to destroy the earth."

12. And God said, "This is the sign of the covenant which I make between me and you and every living creature that is with you, for all future generations:

13. I set my bow in the cloud, and it shall be a sign of the covenant between me and the earth.

14. When I bring clouds over the earth and the bow is seen in the clouds,

15. I will remember my covenant which is between me and you and every living creature of all flesh; and the waters shall never again become a flood to destroy all flesh.

16. When the bow is in the clouds, I will look upon it and remember the everlasting covenant between God and every living creature of all flesh that is upon the earth."

17. God said to Noah, "This is the sign of the covenant which I have established between me and all flesh that is upon the earth."

14.

"I establish my covenant with you."

A year or two ago there was an article in Time Magazine under the title "Are the Bible Stories True?" It was basically about archaeology and its discoveries and the debate which was ongoing among the historians. It also tried to cover the debate between those who studied the stories of other nations in the area and the Old Testament. It was interesting but nothing new was said in the article. In fact, I have to say that I was more interested in the title than in the article. "Are the Bible stories true?"

There used to be a programme on the radio called "The Brains Trust" and only one of the regular contributors was Professor C. E. M. Joad and he began nearly every answer he was trying to give with the words, "It depends what you mean by..." in this case it would be "true". We take the story of Noah and the Ark which we find in Genesis 9. Modern thinking wants to see Noah's birth certificate and his captain's licence, navigational maps and catering arrangements and what we can rediscover about the extent of the flood. Without this information it is not realistic to examine its truth claims. Without this information they would find it difficult to call the story true. But while we might be proud of being modern and having critical criteria to assess its truth or note, we have to remind ourselves that our fellow human beings who were alive at the time of the story would never have thought of asking about its truth value. They would ask a different and, to my mind, a more productive question – "What does the story mean?" And they asked this because it was so obviously a tale of the imagination – they could see the difficulties of keeping lions and gazelles in the same confined area – and also did Noah take two butterflies or two of each species of butterfly? The story gives rise to such questions. And also, did the flood and the ark serve its purpose – was the world a better place after the flood or not?

There's a story of a bishop of the Russian Orthodox Church visiting one of his parishes and telling this story, and a lady asked him why evil persisted in the world after the flood. He answered that while Noah was busy building the ark his wife constantly pestered him and would not accept his invitation to come on board. When the rain became serious and the flood appeared Noah, frustrated at his wife's attitude, shouted at her and indicating the wetness said, "Now you see – so come in, you devil." And the devil accepted his invitation as well as his wife and that is how evil continued after the flood! I have a friend who is a religious education teacher in a secondary school – and, not unusually, there are more classes than he can cover so other members of staff have to help out. He discovered what one of his colleagues was teaching and had to ask the Rector to take him off the job – he was actually telling first year pupils if they did not believe the Noah story totally they would go to Hell! Needless to say he was quickly removed.

It is worth our while noting that the Noah story is one of a kind. It was an area prone to flooding. (You may be interested to know that there was also a flood story by the Welsh Druids to the effect that Britain was flooded and repopulated by the Welsh!) But the Noah story is distinct. In Babylon the story is that the gods were angry because of the noise humans were making so they caused a flood to get rid of them. Remember the passage in I Kings 18 when Elijah taunts the priests of Baal – "perhaps your god is asleep". Israel's God, on the other hand, is He of whom they can say, "He that keepeth thee never sleeps." But in Noah's story it is nothing so petty as a disturbed snooze – it is man's sinfulness that is the problem. God is a moral God who hates sin. His requirement of humanity is a moral requirement and this is a consistent requirement not anything erratic.

In the midst of this world of sin God found Noah. The name means "He who brings relief" – we see Noah as righteous but not perfect but one whose attitude was right – there was a fundamental goodness about him and this was due to the place he gave to God in his life – in other words, his faith. This is different from the Babylon approach – their search for God is not for goodness but the search for eternal youth.

The story ends with God committing Himself – "I establish my covenant with you." This is quite unlike the Babylon stories where the gods, having stopped the noise, let the land dry out – then start again maybe not because of the noise – but the smell – the eating habits – the untidiness – no consistency except for punishing.

We return then to the question – "Are the Bible stories true?"

We've already seen that in the narrow modern sense the answer is "No." And for the Christian the measure of truth is not the fashion of the moment – but Jesus. And Jesus shows us in reality what Noah could only do in imagination. He shows us a moral, loving God who hates sin. He shows us what perfect faith can achieve – he even prays for our forgiveness as he was crucified. And he showed us a God who will defeat sin by love no matter how long it takes. This is something much more profound than a truth we can prove by the cleverness of our thinking. This is something to live by – it's the experience of the saints that the more we learn to live in the grace of the God who establishes his covenant with us the more sense it makes and the more profound is the truth of it.

LUKE 4: 16-30

16. And he came to Nazareth, where he had been brought up; and he went to the synagogue, as his custom was, on the Sabbath day. And he stood up to read;

17. And there was given to him the book of the prophet Isaiah. He opened the book and found the place where it was written,

18. "The Spirit of the Lord is upon me, because he has anointed me to preach good news to the poor. He has sent me to proclaim release to the captives and recovering of sight to the blind, to set at liberty those who are oppressed,

19. To proclaim the acceptable year of the Lord."

20. And he closed the book, and gave it back to the attendant, and sat down; and the eyes of all in the synagogue were fixed on him.

21. And he began to say to them, "Today this scripture has been fulfilled in your hearing."

22. And all spoke well of him, and wondered at the gracious words which proceeded out of his mouth; and they said, "Is not this Joseph's son?"

23. And he said to them, "Doubtless you will quote to me this proverb, 'Physician, heal yourself; what we have heard you did at Caper'na-um, do here also in your own country.'"

24. And he said, "Truly, I say to you, no prophet is acceptable in his own country.

25. But in truth, I tell you, there were many widows in Israel in the days of Eli'jah, when the heaven was shut up three years and six months, when there came a great famine over all the land;

26. And Eli'jah was sent to none of them but only to

Zar'ephath, in the land of Sidon, to a woman who was a widow.

27. And there were many lepers in Israel in the time of the prophet Eli'sha; and none of them was cleansed, but only Na'aman the Syrian."

28. When they heard this, all in the synagogue were filled with wrath.

29. And they rose up and put him out of the city, and led him to the brow of the hill on which their city was built, that they might throw him down headlong.

30. But passing through the midst of them he went away.

15.

"Jesus closed the book."

It sounds like a simple statement of fact – "Jesus closed the book" – and, of course it is. This was the practice in the synagogue. With ceremony, reverence, and dignity the scroll was brought out of its cupboard and the reader opened it and proceeded to read the passage. Then the scroll was rolled up again and replaced in its cupboard to await its next reading. So, Jesus was following the traditional practice. But really, there is a bit more to it than this. Jesus had just read a passage from Isaiah. So the book he closed was the scroll of Isaiah. But it was also the Old Testament. So the book he closed was the Old Testament itself. Thus, we have to look a bit deeper and see if there is something more symbolic here.

Before going into the temple to teach, St Luke tells us Jesus was being tempted in the wilderness. You'll remember there were three temptations: "Turn this stone to bread", "worship the tempter", and "cast yourself down from the pinnacle of the temple."

Jesus' reply on each occasion was, "It is written that man does not live by bread alone; you shall worship only God and serve him," and, "you shall worship only God and serve him." Now each of these is in fact a quotation from the book of Deuteronomy. Deuteronomy has been described as the most spiritual book of the Old Testament. The word "Deuteronomy" means "second law" and it is really best seen as a working out of the ten commandments. It's a remarkable book and points to the very best understanding of the law and is way ahead of its time. It even has laws about the treatment of animals. "Thou shalt not muzzle the mouth of the Ox when he treadeth out the corn." By quoting Deuteronomy Jesus showed he was fulfilling the law. But by closing the book Jesus was showing he was going beyond the law. Law is always limited; it tells us what not to do and gives out punishment for transgression. Jesus wants to show that there is more to life than this – he wants to replace the laws with compassion, forgiveness, and above all, love. The book is closed so that a new book may be opened.

As we saw, it was the book of Isaiah that Jesus closed. As Deuteronomy was the law at its highest point, so Isaiah was prophecy at its highest point and most perceptive: "a man of sorrows and acquainted with grief", "surely he has borne our griefs", and "our iniquities were placed upon him." Jesus used these Isaiah thoughts as a model for his own life and message, thus ensuring recognition for his teaching (don't fall into the trap of thinking that in some way Isaiah, or any prophet, had foreknowledge of what would happen in the future). If you think about that you're thinking that Jesus was in some way predetermined and therefore not free! Love which is not free is not love, it's coercion. No. Instead the role of the suffering servant – the one who volunteered to pay the price of our sins was freely chosen by Jesus and in so choosing he fulfilled the prophecy and closed the book. "This day these words are fulfilled in your presence."

In closing the book of the law and the prophets Jesus opened the book of the Gospels – the new book – the New Testament. The Old Testament is occupied by sin and its consequences. In the wilderness Jesus showed how to conquer sin and temptation. This cannot be said often enough – "JESUS OVERCAME SIN" and in so doing showed that it was not inevitable, it doesn't need to happen. It happens because of our weakness, stupidity, lack of faith and simple cussedness. But Jesus showed it's not necessary. If you like, he closed the book on sin. Critics of the Christian faith pour scorn on God for being so slow in bringing his creation to perfection. It's not God who is slow – it is us! We choose to go on sinning even though Jesus showed it is not necessary. Jesus closed the book, namely the book on sin! God is very patient, he has in Jesus closed the book on sin – and so far we have not proceeded beyond Chapter 1!

The other aspect of the Old Testament was that in contrast to the paganism roundabout, it saw God as exalted. The word most often used of God is HOLY. And in the Old Testament the word used for HOLY means "APART" And there were times when they saw God as so holy – so "apart" – that he was unapproachable. Jesus, on the other hand, without in any way compromising God's holiness brought him back to humanity – "the very hairs of your head are numbered – even the sparrows are known by him."

Isaiah said at one point, "Verily thou art a God

that hidest thyself." Jesus' Father did not hide but was shown by Jesus to be present and available to us in all times and places. Jesus closed the book on this God who could only be seen as holy and high and exalted and made him known to us as a Father who loves us with a love we have hardly begun to understand.

Jesus closed the book. A very symbolic event and as we have seen a very suggestive happening. Yet ultimately it does not say enough – it has that tinge of the negative about it – closed – finished with – put away. And one thing we can be sure of is that there is never anything negative about Jesus. If Jesus closed the book it was to offer us something more positive. And that is what he does – he brings us to the new book – the book of his life and teaching and his suffering for our sake, his healing and his sacrifice – the new book of life with God our Maker.

PHILIPPIANS 2: 1-11

1. So if there is any encouragement in Christ, any incentive of love, any participation in the Spirit, any affection and sympathy,

2. Complete my joy by being of the same mind, having the same love, being in full accord and of one mind.

3. Do nothing from selfishness or conceit, but in humility count others better than yourselves.

4. Let each of you look not only to his own interests, but also to the interests of others.

5. Have this mind among yourselves, which is yours in Christ Jesus,

6. Who, though he was in the form of God, did not count equality with God a thing to be grasped,

7. But emptied himself, taking the form of a servant, being born in the likeness of men.

8. And being found in human form he humbled himself and became obedient unto death, even death on a cross.

9. Therefore God has highly exalted him and bestowed on him the name which is above every name,

10. That at the name of Jesus every knee should bow, in heaven and on earth and under the earth,

11. And every tongue confess that Jesus Christ is Lord, to the glory of God the Father.

16.

"Let this mind be in you which was also in Christ Jesus."

The eminent philosopher and scholar, A C Grayling, recently published (2011 to be precise) an interesting book entitled *The Good Book*. He subtitles it "a secular bible". He declares that he aspires to guide us through the "paths of the wise, master thinkers whose mighty works are monuments to posterity" and he seeks by means of these thinkers, "resources to promote what is true and good." This, of course, invites the question: who does Professor Grayling count as being wise? The reviewer of the book in the Daily Telegraph, Genevieve Fox, was disappointed with it; simple, she said, "it fails to convince." He gives a list of the so-called 'wise.' But he misses out: Moses who gave us the Ten Commandments, still often looked at in the secular world as a good foundation for law makers. Indeed, I don't think he mentions any Biblical personnel. He ignores Jesus whose beatitudes still point the way to good human living and understanding of our nature. His total atheism has left him blinkered, and I have to say, it compromises his scholarship. For example, he lists as one of his so-called sources of wisdom Immanuel Kant. Kant was a very analytical philosopher and was thorough in his writing to present his thoughts in the least ambiguous way. In his famous "groundwork of the metaphysic of morals" Kant at one point states: "Even the Holy One of our Gospels cannot command love." In other words, even Kant acknowledges that there is a "beyond" that cannot be reached "within the limits of human thinking alone." Suffice it to say that while the arch-priest of atheism, Richard Dawkins, he does not compromise his atheism but still acknowledges Jesus as a moral teacher. It has to be said that such closed-mindedness is likely to result in a less than acceptable outcome. Here is an example: Grayling writes, "It is our attitude to things that give them their value, whether good or bad or indifferent." Taken to its conclusion this means, if I don't like something it has no value! On the whole this good book is a disappointment. Can we do better?

I recall in the early 1960s sitting in the College Church of Aberdeen University. The preacher was Dr Archie Craig of Glasgow University who was that year moderator of the General Assembly of the Church of Scotland. He was telling us the story of Job and his so-called "comforters." Dr Craig examined the comfort that Job was offered and how in one way or another it wasn't very comforting. And I remember vividly to this day his words. "Job's comforters did their best to make sense of his tragic experiences, one by one they offered their wisdom, and, though well-intended, it fell short of what was needed: so comforter one spoke, then comforter two, then comforter three, but then God spoke, and when God spoke, he changed the subject." Whenever God speaks he changes the subject! This was a call to look beyond – there's more to humanity than the wisdom of wise! We don't just need a God to fill the gaps in our knowledge – we need a God, not of our invention but a God who reveals himself in changing the subject!

On another occasion, it was the same man who once more gave us a pointer to understand our faith. At the Church of Scotland General Assembly – again in the 1960s – the report of the Church and Nation Committee was being debated. The Very Reverend George MacLeod was speaking on the matter of nuclear weapons. Dr MacLeod was a very passionate speaker and this occasion was no different. When he sat down Dr Archie Craig also spoke to the issue. He said that he had listened carefully to his colleague and that he concluded that to follow Dr MacLeod was to be simplistic and ignore the dangers of living in the modern world. It was to give up our last line of defence and leave ourselves open to aggression. And he continued pointing out all the weakening consequences of doing away with the bombs. Then he dropped his own bombshell by saying that for all these reasons he agreed with Dr MacLeod and would support his motion – because, he said, "I hear therein the authentic voice of Jesus Christ." These men were both heroes – they both held the Military Cross for bravery and Dr MacLeod also had the Croix de Guerre. And here they were wanting to give away our defensive deterrent weapons because this action represented what was to their minds "the authentic voice of Jesus Christ."

Jesus was a toughie! He faced his accusers fearlessly. The late Professor James S Stewart used to say to his students (all male in his day), "For God's sake gentlemen do not make the name of Jesus sweet and sickly." Jesus faced the cross rather than resort to a false defence. He refused to let the rulers of the world dictate his terms. And he preached and practised love. And practising the Jesus kind of love is hard and demanding – forgive those who abuse you! Really! But practising the authentic words of Jesus can mean swallowing pride – "Give gentle answers back again and fight a battle for the Lord."

We asked the question following our look at Professor Grayling's book, "Can we do better?" We can talk of a God who knows our humanity, weaknesses and all – yet if we listen He will change the subject and turn our weakness into strength. And there's Jesus, who will show us the way to conquer self and practise love and forgiveness. These are ruled out by Grayling from the outset.

There's a story in the book of Exodus chapter 5 – the Israelites were in captivity in Egypt and fell foul of Pharaoh's command, so they were told that from then on they had to make their bricks "without straw." This made their work more difficult and the end product less strong. The phrase "bricks without straw" has made its way into our language and is used to describe an effort without the requisite resources. Professor Grayling has attempted the task of making us wiser and better, but he fails because his exclusive atheism is making bricks without straw.

Let us rejoice that we have a God who changes the subject and a Lord the authenticity of whose voice shows us always how we should live. Let this mind be in us which is also in Jesus.

Zechariah 8: 3 and Luke 9: 57-62

ZECHARIAH 8: 3

3. Thus says the Lord: I will return to Zion, and will dwell in the midst of Jerusalem, and Jerusalem shall be called the faithful city, and the mountain of the Lord of hosts, the holy mountain.

LUKE 9: 57-62

57. As they were going along the road, a man said to him, "I will follow you wherever you go."

58. And Jesus said to him, "Foxes have holes, and birds of the air have nests; but the Son of man has nowhere to lay his head."

59. To another he said, "Follow me." But he said, "Lord, let me first go and bury my father."

60. But he said to him, "Leave the dead to bury their own dead; but as for you, go and proclaim the kingdom of God."

61. Another said, "I will follow you, Lord; but let me first say farewell to those at my home."

62. Jesus said to him, "No one who puts his hand to the plow and looks back is fit for the kingdom of God."

17.

"Let us go with you for we have heard that God is with you."

It's hardly news to us that Church membership is declining. From time to time our newspapers print a story which tells us how much the decline is and how few people regularly attend Church. And the conclusion drawn is that we are now in a minority. Apparently only one in seven of us now attend Church with any degree of regularity and fewer than a third of the population belong to a Church – and this number is falling; as the older people die off they are not replaced by the new generation. Gone are the days when the Churches were full and when in numerical terms we could be called a Christian country, though that was always based on the dubious assumption that to attend Church was to be a Christian.

We can perhaps think of some of the reasons given as to why this is so. It is suggested that humanity has outgrown the need for religion. Our advances in knowledge have made much of what religion has to say more and more incredible – indeed some suggest mumbo jumbo is how many see the better description of what religion teaches than anything else. But, this explanation does not really square with the facts. There are more people than ever today who consult their horoscopes. From time to time, an event occurs that gives rise to a reaction that resembles pandemonium – such as when a couple of Hindu statues appear to have absorbed a drop or two of milk! I hear that some people actually phone astrologers to pick their lottery numbers. So, far from outgrowing religion, we seem sometimes to be going back to a more primitive form.

It's advanced by some modern gurus that we can be moral without being religious – so we don't need religion to keep us good. I'm sure there is a truth here. I'm sure there are some great souls who have managed by their own efforts to reach an admirable standard of purity. But it's hard to think who they are. In fact I would suggest the opposite is the case, namely, the decline in churchgoing is accompanied by a decline in moral standards. Sleaze is a more common word in public life than at any other time in my life. As a society we parade our sexual libertinism as if we have made a new discovery. And self-abuse through drugs and stimulants would make Dickens want to rewrite his novels! No, contemporary morality seems to me more like a car with faulty brakes that is accelerating to a cliff edge.

The Church undoubtedly has a negative image and I'm afraid we have to concede that there's truth in this. Very often the Church has appeared more ready to condemn than it is to love. Very often we seem to be against virtually all kinds of enjoyment and for no particular reason. I very much hope this is something that will pass, although I have to say that the growth of some of the more narrow and fundamentalist groups might increase the negative response. It's important for us to remember that the Church is made up of human members and we make mistakes and we should admit this and ask forgiveness.

At the end of the day there are really no valid reasons why the Church should be in decline. The real truth is that we as a society have opted out. We can fill our lives with other pastimes such as sport and TV so we can do without the Church. But the Christian experience of life leads us to want to say, "We can do without the Church, but we can't do without the Gospel – we need that for the sake of our humanity."

Archbishop William Temple said, "There's a God-shaped hole in mankind." In other words, God made us so that we are aware of our need of something greater than ourselves. If we don't fill this hole properly then something else will fill it – superstition that leads to darkness, that leads to prejudice, that leads to ethnic cleansing, etc. We need the Gospel to save us from that. We need the morality of the Gospel – without it, society crumbles – look at our divorce and illegitimacy rate – look at the incidents of child abuse – lack of self-control, lack of discipline. These are the basics of morality but they demonstrate a lack of love for those who trust us. And what the Gospel has to offer is a morality of love and we've hardly started on that road. We need to recover the positive healing of Jesus. Look how time and time again he astounded the scribes and Pharisees of his time – i.e. the wise men. Of course he was against some things – hypocrisy and greed – what's wrong with being against that? He was also against what corrupted, but his message was always positive – forgive – love – forgive again and love again. We need the Gospel for its positive teaching and its vision of what human beings can be when they give their lives to following him.

Zechariah had a high opinion of his faith. "Let us go with you for we have heard that God is with you." The Church may be in decline but don't let that put you off. Be proud of your faith, practise it more and harder and try to let Jesus' love be your motivation. The decline should mean the half-hearted have gone away and we read in St Luke "they were not yet fit for the Kingdom!" We pray for them and hope they will see their loss. But if those of us who are left share Zechariah's vision and live our faith then its attractiveness will be seen and that's the best sermon of all. Michael Buerk, the BBC reporter who brought the world the horrendous famine in Ethiopia expressed in his autobiography "The road taken" his attitude to religion – he has no religion personally. But he states that time and again when he meets some Christians he admires their lovely courtesy. That's a lovely compliment – the Christian faith is a religion of courtesy – and courtesy is just a small step from love. Be proud to be a Christian.

MATTHEW 5: 13-20

13. "You are the salt of the earth; but if salt has lost its taste, how shall its saltness be restored? It is no longer good for anything except to be thrown out and trodden under foot by men.

14. "You are the light of the world. A city set on a hill cannot be hid.

15. Nor do men light a lamp and put it under a bushel, but on a stand, and it gives light to all in the house.

16. Let your light so shine before men, that they may see your good works and give glory to your Father who is in heaven.

17. "Think not that I have come to abolish the law and the prophets; I have come not to abolish them but to fulfil them.

18. For truly, I say to you, till heaven and earth pass away, not an iota, not a dot, will pass from the law until all is accomplished.

19. Whoever then relaxes one of the least of these commandments and teaches men so, shall be called least in the kingdom of heaven; but he who does them and teaches them shall be called great in the kingdom of heaven.

20. For I tell you, unless your righteousness exceeds that of the scribes and Phar'isees, you will never enter the kingdom of heaven.

18.

"Let your light so shine before men, that they may see your good works and give glory to your father who is in Heaven."

I read the story of a young boy who was taken to Church by his parents from an early age. He sat and looked at all that was there – a communion table, a baptismal font – the organ with all its stops and pipes, and the building itself with its high roof and coloured windows. After a few weeks he had asked all the usual questions – but I'm told he looked at and pointed to the stained-glass windows and asked his parents "are those the adverts?" Unknowingly he was wiser than he thought – these windows can be the showcase of the Church's aims and teaching. Many times the windows are a reminder of the Biblical stories. I recall a holiday in Austria – a Catholic country – and visiting the Churches in the mountain villages – almost without exception the main window was a picture of the Virgin and child. They were very beautiful and well cared for and they certainly pointed to the Christmas story. And many Churches have windows like this and I'm sure they add colour to the act of worship. But I have a greater liking for windows which draw our attention to the works and thinking of some of the great followers of Jesus and how they made his Gospel alive and relevant.

One such is the 7th Earl of Shaftsbury – Anthony Ashley Cooper. He was an unwanted child, his parents showed him no love – he was merely an accident of marriage and he was left in the care of a nanny – Maria Millis. Maria was a devout Christian and she taught young Anthony the Gospel message and taught him how to pray and made known to him what living in the way of Jesus' Gospel meant. And he grew up to make the implementation of that Gospel his life's work. He became a Member of Parliament and one of the hardest working Parliamentarians. He saw the situation in many of the working-class areas as uncivilised and even cruel: Young boys being pushed up chimneys to sweep them; young children of both sexes sent down mines in long shifts of darkness and danger as well as insanitary. He saw children growing into adulthood without schooling. And he was well aware in the London of his day there was no proper sewage system. There was inadequate provision for the care of the insane. And he cast his eye beyond the mid-19th century Britain – he looked to India and practice of "suttee", the cremation of widows to accompany their husband in the after-life. He worked for the reform of seamen's contracts to give them decent conditions and a reasonable home life. He turned his attention to the Church, particularly the Church of England, where many of the vicars drew the stipends and did very little, and often did not live in the parish which was in the gift of an uncle or suchlike. He was also president of the

Bible Society and worked to make the scripture stories known. His life of parliamentary laws is awesome: employment laws of a maximum working week: children's employment laws – the foundation of Ragged Schools – employment laws of a maximum working week – care of the insane – and civic responsibility for proper sanitation. On his death, a statue was erected in the centre of London. It is popularly known as Eros – the god of love – but in fact it was Anteros – the angel of charity. Interestingly the statue was lifted during the Second World War and placed in a safe-keeping position. At the end of the war it was replaced but with the arrow in the bow pointing up Shaftsbury Avenue – towards his home. Prior to this it had its arrow pointing towards the House of Commons. (There are many who think it was better pointing to the Commons to remind them of their duty!) Alas, there is no stained-glass window for Maria Millis! But, interestingly, there is a memorial window to Lord Anthony in the city hall in Belfast. When a Christian does his work well it is recognised and lauded beyond the Church.

Another great Christian witness and worker was the eminent theologian Dietrich Bonhoeffer. In one of his writings about the situation in Germany under Hitler he wrote: "if you are on a bus and it is evident that the driver is drunk your duty is to get him away from the wheel as soon as possible." He wrote to the Church beyond Germany, in particular to a Swedish bishop he knew well, telling what his country was like. In one of his famous books he writes of "cheap grace" and "costly grace". Cheap grace is getting the benediction on Sunday and that's that. Costly grace is where you stand up for your faith against all who drag society and the world downwards. And he practised costly grace and for his opposition to Hitler he had the most horrendous execution – he was hanged with wire! He said before his death: "this is the end: for me the beginning of life." Bonhoeffer has several memorials but he has a stained-glass window in St David's Basilica Church in Berlin. I ask, how many other traitors do you know who have a stained-glass window in their memory in their country's capital city? This is what costly grace can achieve in the name of Jesus.

On the 15th September 1963 in the 16th Street Baptist Church in Birmingham, Alabama (USA), a bomb was shot through the Church window and killed four young black girls at worship. The Church was the meeting place for nonviolent civil rights activists – but obviously to the Ku Klux Klan, a threat. The news of this barbarism broke on worldwide news programmes and a Welsh artist by the name of John Petts was determined to do something about it. So, he set about designing and making an appropriate stained glass window. To raise the cost he asked his fellow Welsh people to make a donation but he did not want it to be a gift from wealthy people only so he asked for donations not exceeding half a crown (in old money an eighth of a pound). The money was widely raised and the new window installed: it shows an anguished man in a crucifixion position. But the man is black! One lady in the Church said, "We didn't know that black people mattered!" To this day the window is there and the story is told. It is called the Wales Window. It proclaims in its own way that evil must never flourish.

The little boy in his innocence got it right when he

saw them as adverts. They advertise in pictures what Jesus was and did, and they encourage us to follow him as best we can.

Luke 11: 1-13 and Genesis 32: 22-32

LUKE 11: 1-13

1. He was praying in a certain place, and when he ceased, one of his disciples said to him, "Lord, teach us to pray, as John taught his disciples."

2. And he said to them, "When you pray, say: "Father, hallowed be thy name. Thy kingdom come.

3. Give us each day our daily bread;

4. And forgive us our sins, for we ourselves forgive every one who is indebted to us; and lead us not into temptation."

5. And he said to them, "Which of you who has a friend will go to him at midnight and say to him, 'Friend, lend me three loaves;

6. For a friend of mine has arrived on a journey, and I have nothing to set before him';

7. And he will answer from within, 'Do not bother me; the door is now shut, and my children are with me in bed; I cannot get up and give you anything'?

8. I tell you, though he will not get up and give him anything because he is his friend, yet because of his importunity he will rise and give him whatever he needs.

9. And I tell you, Ask, and it will be given you; seek, and you will find; knock, and it will be opened to you.

10. For every one who asks receives, and he who seeks finds, and to him who knocks it will be opened.

11. What father among you, if his son asks for a fish, will instead of a fish give him a serpent;

12. Or if he asks for an egg, will give him a scorpion?

13. If you then, who are evil, know how to give good gifts to your children, how much more will the heavenly Father give the Holy Spirit to those who ask him!"

GENESIS 32: 22-32

22. The same night he arose and took his two wives, his two maids, and his eleven children, and crossed the ford of the Jabbok.

23. He took them and sent them across the stream, and likewise everything that he had.

24. And Jacob was left alone; and a man wrestled with him until the breaking of the day.

25. When the man saw that he did not prevail against Jacob, he touched the hollow of his thigh; and Jacob's thigh was put out of joint as he wrestled with him.

26. Then he said, "Let me go, for the day is breaking." But Jacob said, "I will not let you go, unless you bless me."

27. And he said to him, "What is your name?" And he said, "Jacob."

28. Then he said, "Your name shall no more be called Jacob, but Israel, for you have striven with God and with men, and have prevailed."

29. Then Jacob asked him, "Tell me, I pray, your name." But he said, "Why is it that you ask my name?" And there he blessed him.

30. So Jacob called the name of the place Penu'el, saying, "For I have seen God face to face, and yet my life is preserved."

31. The sun rose upon him as he passed Penu'el, limping because of his thigh.

32. Therefore to this day the Israelites do not eat the sinew of the hip which is upon the hollow of the thigh, because he touched the hollow of Jacob's thigh on the sinew of the hip.

19.

"Lord teach us to pray as John taught his disciples."

A Church in an area where I used to work became vacant when the incumbent minister retired. It was a Church in an industrial area but with a decline in some of the industries there was quite a degree of unemployment and consequently a shortage of money. The result was that the Church had failed to pay its way and had accumulated quite an amount of debt. After much discussion it was decided that an area of the size this Church covered was just too large to integrate with another congregation, and, therefore, they should recruit another minister. But it was made clear the new minister should be made aware that there was such a debt and be prepared to work to improve the finances. Of the applicants one minister in particular attracted them and he was forthright about his attitude to the debt. He said firmly that he would deal with the debt by means of prayer! And he managed to convince the congregation that he was the man for the job. So he duly became the new minister and after an appropriate introductory period he informed the congregation that he was ready to fulfil his promise and deal with the debt by means of prayer and this would be done on the first Saturday of the coming month. Notices would be put in shop windows, letters sent home with school pupils, and other organisations such as bowling clubs, etc., would receive the information. Then he told them his idea – he was going to hold a day of sponsored prayer. He himself would be in the Church from 8 a.m. to 8 p.m. and invited sponsorship by the hour. He would also welcome anyone who had a concern to come to him in the Church and he would pray with them – and, of course, if it was accompanied by a donation, so much the better. I am fairly sure this came as a surprise to the congregation who did not think that this was how his promise would be understood. And I also imagine some complications – a dear granny wanting her grandson to pass his English exam asks a prayer and gives an offering. Does she get her money back if he fails? Be that as it may, he went ahead with his plan and reduced the debt considerably. A day or two later I met a lady who was a member of that Church. "Did you hear about our minister? Wasn't it good! I think I'll try, my premium bond might come up." You can tell this is a few years ago – today, I suspect, it would be "my lotto ticket might come up." But let's look at it.

"I think I'll try that." That is an admission that she does not pray regularly. I wonder how many of our Church members fall into that category? I suspect quite a few, and as with many things admitting it can be the beginning of putting it right. The minister to whom I was assistant many years ago was a wise man. He insisted that as well as the regular necessary committee meetings there should also be meetings of the same people but not for business. There should be time for, for example, looking at the work of the Church in the nation, for example in eventide homes, in overseas work and so on. These were well attended and much appreciated. I recall one such meeting when there was to be a discussion on what it meant to be a member of the Church. Various topics were raised, including prayer. One of the most senior members caused a surprise by saying, "I gave up on prayer a long time ago – I found it too difficult." There was a drawing of breath, because this was a man we all regarded as an example of what a Christian should be – a thorough gentleman, sober and excellent in his home and work life. And of course, it led to a similar admission from quite a few others. The consensus was "prayer is hard". This, I have to say is a good place to begin.

St Augustine, for example, said, "ORARE EST LABORARE" – "prayer is work." And Mother Teresa said, "Most of prayer is not words – but listening." Professor Murdo Ewan MacDonald, the well-known preacher here in Scotland, loved to tell the story from his prisoner-of-war days. With his fellow prisoners he was being transported from one Gulag to another by train when an RAF bomber started to drop bombs on their train – and fortunately for them there was no direct hit. Afterwards his travelling companions rebuked him for sitting reading during the air raid – their complaint was that he just sat and read his book while they all prayed furiously that the bombs would miss.

"Why did you not pray?" they asked.

His reply was that he had already prayed at the beginning of the day, and added, "I do not wait for the emergency!"

A Scottish minister, Andrew Bonnar, in the 19th century wrote a kind of spiritual autobiography. He tells how he resolved to say the Lord's prayer meaningfully by telling one piece at a time and not moving on until he knew he had understood it. He records, "Today I got as far as 'thy kingdom come' – then I got as far as 'on earth'." His diary thus goes on until the entry, "I have realised the difficulty of the task I have set myself and will have to be content just to do the best I can."

"Prayer is hard" – in Genesis 24 we learn that Jacob after praying walked with a limp – let's hope for his sake it was an intellectual limp – but it makes the point.

The disciples in St Luke 11 ask Jesus "teach us to pray." It needs to be learned – and like all worthwhile agendas – it's hard. We find that in prayer we are like infants before our father's God. But, let's stop and think. How many falls do we have as infants learning to walk? How many words do we muddle when we are learning to talk – 'baby' words. Is it surprising that our adult spiritual bones get hurt when we attempt something so difficult – and yet – so rewarding.

Let us admit what our prayer is like – or not like. Let us acknowledge the difficulty that puts us off. But let us learn from our fellow Christians who have somehow managed to make prayer meaningful that it is worth keeping on.

As a minister I am often asked about prayer and have no easy answer. I find more and more that I suggest the hymn book as a starter. Simply but earnestly read a hymn – any one – most are good. Then stop and think about it – let it speak to you – let it tell you how to think about our God – Father – Saviour – Companion. So what if, like the babe learning to walk, we tumble and feel foolish? That is part of physical growing – prayer is nothing other than spiritual growing.

1 CORINTHIANS 12: 1-30

1. Now concerning spiritual gifts, brethren, I do not want you to be uninformed.

2. You know that when you were heathen, you were led astray to dumb idols, however you may have been moved.

3. Therefore I want you to understand that no one speaking by the Spirit of God ever says "Jesus be cursed!" and no one can say "Jesus is Lord" except by the Holy Spirit.

4. Now there are varieties of gifts, but the same Spirit;

5. And there are varieties of service, but the same Lord;

6. And there are varieties of working, but it is the same God who inspires them all in every one.

7. To each is given the manifestation of the Spirit for the common good.

8. To one is given through the Spirit the utterance of wisdom, and to another the utterance of knowledge according to the same Spirit,

9. To another faith by the same Spirit, to another gifts of healing by the one Spirit,

10. To another the working of miracles, to another prophecy, to another the ability to distinguish between spirits, to another various kinds of tongues, to another the interpretation of tongues.

11. All these are inspired by one and the same Spirit, who apportions to each one individually as he wills.

12. For just as the body is one and has many members, and all the members of the body, though many, are one body, so it is with Christ.

13. For by one Spirit we were all baptized into one body—Jews or Greeks, slaves or free—and all were made to drink of one Spirit.

14. For the body does not consist of one member but of many.

15. If the foot should say, "Because I am not a hand, I do not belong to the body," that would not make it any less a part of the body.

16. And if the ear should say, "Because I am not an eye, I do not belong to the body," that would not make it any less a part of the body.

17. If the whole body were an eye, where would be the hearing? If the whole body were an ear, where would be the sense of smell?

18. But as it is, God arranged the organs in the body, each one of them, as he chose.

19. If all were a single organ, where would the body be?

20. As it is, there are many parts, yet one body.

21. The eye cannot say to the hand, "I have no need of you," nor again the head to the feet, "I have no need of you."

22. On the contrary, the parts of the body which seem to be weaker are indispensable,

23. And those parts of the body which we think less honourable we invest with the greater honour, and our unpresentable parts are treated with greater modesty,

24. Which our more presentable parts do not require. But God has so composed the body, giving the greater honour to the inferior part,

25. That there may be no discord in the body, but that the members may have the same care for one another.

26. If one member suffers, all suffer together; if one member is honoured, all rejoice together.

27. Now you are the body of Christ and individually members of it.

28. And God has appointed in the church first apostles, second prophets, third teachers, then workers of miracles, then healers, helpers, administrators, speakers in various kinds of tongues.

29. Are all apostles? Are all prophets? Are all teachers? Do all work miracles?

30. Do all possess gifts of healing? Do all speak with tongues? Do all interpret?

20.

"Now there are variations of gifts but the same Spirit."

Time and time again, watching nature programmes on television I have to confess that quite often I express surprise. There is, apparently, a breed of duck that lives its total life inside the Arctic Circle. For a long time biologists have known about this duck and its habitat but never really understood how it could survive such extreme temperatures. It always seemed healthy enough. In relatively modern times with better research facilities it has been discovered that the duck had a secret – it keeps its feathers which keep it warm from freezing by means of anti-freeze! It has the ability to secrete a sufficient volume and thus enables its feathers to keep their warmth-giving function going – and so they survive. Anti-freeze in a duck!

We know, or think we do, that the function of an ear – mainly in mammals – is to enable us to hear, and from time to time be aware of danger when we hear loud sounds and so avoid the danger. Yet, an elephant has ears that are much larger than other mammals. But surely the elephant doesn't need such large ears to keep it safe by receiving noises that signify danger. However, on closer examination it has been discovered that the elephant's ear is in fact a kind of air-conditioning unit. The ear as we see it is in fact full of capillaries which carry the blood to its surface from whence, after cooling, it can be returned into the blood circulation and perform its function without overheating the vast internal area of the animal.

Anti-freeze in the arctic: air conditioning in the heat of Africa. The appropriate biological response to the environment. These are the gifts of nature to its inhabitants. And of course we can find many more. But it is a truth that what we find in nature we find too in the life of the spirit. St Paul often referred to the gifts of the spirit – God's gifts to human creatures. In fact we can say that this is one of St Paul's favourite themes but he is careful that we have to see these gifts are all from the same source. It is important that we remember this otherwise we are in danger of falling into quackery! There is a group of so-called Churches who name themselves 'the Church of Jesus Christ' with signs following – and they prove, or try to prove their faith by handling poisonous snakes, and the fact that they do not get poisoned themselves is proof of their faith. I don't think that Paul would approve – he talks about gifts being given to us for "the common good." (I Corinthians 12 v 7) We ask, what is the common good in handling a snake? St Paul also mentions the gift of tongues. This is a gift which many find embarrassing. In a fit of enthusiasm some people seem to give way to expressing themselves in unintelligible mutterings. The trouble with this is that it can be artificial – so we have to remind ourselves that the way we are to judge gifts is by asking how they contribute to the common good. If a hip-hip hooray, or a hallelujah raise the spirits of a congregation, good and well – otherwise no thank you.

There is a story of an Evangelical choir from the USA touring Britain and conducting Church services. The minister leading them would conduct the service and preach the sermon. Seemingly at an evening service in the city of Glasgow, the sermon was attracting attention but no response. This was in the days when the Beadle wore a robe and with all dignity carried the Bible in at the start of the service. Well, the choir master didn't have such dignity and encouraged members of the choir to emphasise the minister's preaching with a loud 'Hallelujah' or a 'Praise the Lord.' This was obviously more than the dignity of the Beadle could stand, so he came from his pew and stood in front of the choir and made the announcement, "This is a Presbyterian Church in the city of Glasgow on a Sabbath evening – we'll have no praising of the Lord here if you don't mind!" This indeed expressed the typical solemnity of much of worship – but we are meant not just to be solemnised but to be lifted up – to enjoy and to rejoice in worship. A balance has to be sought, remembering that enthusiasm for God has to be expressed. (The word ENTHUSIASM after all literally means IN-GOD-ISM!)

There is another story of President Abraham Lincoln leaving his guardians on a journey to attend a Church service. On re-joining his entourage he was asked, "What did the preacher preach about?"

Lincoln answered, "Sin."

His companion then asked, "And what did he say?"

Lincoln answered, "He was agin it!"

It was an unknown Victorian man who said, "Having a Calvinist conscience doesn't stop us from doing what we shouldn't – it just stops us enjoying it!"

The gift of tongues should be seen in this context. It is the gift that truly used should help us to "Glorify God and rejoice in him forever." Always for the common good.

The gift of healing – there is alas a wideness here. Healing from a bodily illness, healing from an addiction, healing relationships, healing attitudes, etc. I have, as I'm sure we all have, known people facing death who are reconciled and brave. I have known people with flu who curse their luck and blame everybody. The Gospels use the word "whole". Healing is the gift to ourselves to keep us whole, and a gift we can use to encourage others to find wholeness for themselves by getting to know Jesus and letting him be the agenda for our lives too.

As I said, St Paul liked the theme of God's gifts. We should study them all and look at how they work for the common good.

We do not need anti-freeze – we have not got feathers and most of us have central heating these days. We do not need an air conditioning system – we are not in the tropics. Just as these animal gifts are suitable to their environment – so are his gifts for us.

Suitable to enable us to try to live a Christian life – for the common good. Our secular society needs Christian people to maintain the truth of God's will for us and our world.

ACTS 5: 12-32

12. Now many signs and wonders were done among the people by the hands of the apostles. And they were all together in Solomon's Portico.

13. None of the rest dared join them, but the people held them in high honour.

14. And more than ever believers were added to the Lord, multitudes both of men and women,

15. So that they even carried out the sick into the streets, and laid them on beds and pallets, that as Peter came by at least his shadow might fall on some of them.

16. The people also gathered from the towns around Jerusalem, bringing the sick and those afflicted with unclean spirits, and they were all healed.

17. But the high priest rose up and all who were with him, that is, the party of the Sad'ducees, and filled with jealousy

18. They arrested the apostles and put them in the common prison.

19. But at night an angel of the Lord opened the prison doors and brought them out and said,

20. "Go and stand in the temple and speak to the people all the words of this Life."

21. And when they heard this, they entered the temple at daybreak and taught. Now the high priest came and those who were with him and called together the council and all the senate of Israel, and sent to the prison to have them brought.

22. But when the officers came, they did not find them in the prison, and they returned and reported,

23. "We found the prison securely locked and the sentries standing at the doors, but when we opened it we found no one inside."

24. Now when the captain of the temple and the chief priests heard these words, they were much perplexed about them, wondering what this would come to.

25. And some one came and told them, "The men whom you put in prison are standing in the temple and teaching the people."

26. Then the captain with the officers went and brought them, but without violence, for they were afraid of being stoned by the people.

27. And when they had brought them, they set them before the council. And the high priest questioned them,

28. Saying, "We strictly charged you not to teach in this name, yet here you have filled Jerusalem with your teaching and you intend to bring this man's blood upon us."

29. But Peter and the apostles answered, "We must obey God rather than men.

30. The God of our fathers raised Jesus whom you killed by hanging him on a tree.

31. God exalted him at his right hand as Leader and Saviour, to give repentance to Israel and forgiveness of sins.

32. And we are witnesses to these things, and so is the Holy Spirit whom God has given to those who obey him."

21.

"That Peter's shadow might fall on them."

Many universities and colleges generously do some charitable work and attempt to raise money to help wherever there is need. In a university I attended we had a Rag Week. People sought sponsorship for various nutty stunts and we had a parade through the main street in the town – in lorries disguised in many cases – we had Noah's Ark – and the public were asked to put money in a collection box. It was usually very successful. I recall one year standing in a queue to shake hands with a young lady who was sitting on a decorated chair at the top of a flight of stairs. She was getting a shilling per handshake – because – we got to shake the hand that had shaken the hand of John Lennon of the Beatles. It was, of course, just a bit of fun but it realised a fair sum of money. But it is an observable fact that famous people have an attraction – for good or ill. Maybe there is some talent that they have and we can hope a bit of it will rub off on us. It is documented that soldiers in the Crimean War actually kissed Florence Nightingale's shadow as she went through the wards of the field hospitals – these were battle hardened men.

In a very minor way on Clydeside some years ago – before the lottery – Thursday night seemed to be the night for filling in your football coupon – and I have been asked, believe it or not, to bless a coupon. I made some lame excuse that "my book didn't seem to have a prayer for that." This story of Peter's shadow is telling of a relatively frequent occurrence.

A consideration of the story in the Acts of the Apostles is, of course, rather old. But it speaks of a universal event. Indeed if we look at India with the Caste System, the reverse is true. There are those in India who would not, for example, eat food prepared by or served by an untouchable. We know that the simple fact of being within someone's shadow is really nothing out of the ordinary – yet stubbornly it is still believed by many to be something special.

The same can be said of the people of New Testament times – they may not have had a scientific prejudice but neither did they live in fairyland, some enchanted universe where the laws of nature were broken as a matter of course. In fact the New Testament is very reticent about miracles: we find, for example, Jesus telling those who experienced healing in his presence to go and tell no one (e.g. Matthew 8 v 4). We can reasonably say the New Testament was more interested in what the "event" pointed to rather than the "event" itself. Indeed the Greek term often translated as miracle really means "sign". So what we are being told is that there are events in human life which we can say are such that we may see God at work. These events were never for their own sake but evidences that God does work in our world – if we will let him.

There is no need for there to be an antithesis between science and religion if we are open-minded. We are now recognising that even in science there is much that is believed rather than proved. It may seem a bit odd to suggest that the flap of a butterfly's wing in Aberdeen can be related to the causing of a storm in Brazil – the interconnection of events is only beginning to be looked at. Serendipity is the fortunate coincidence and is probably more common than we recognise.

What the Bible is trying to get us to recognise is that God is at work in our world and can lead us to a new understanding of our experiences – though I would not be prepared to argue that a minister's blessing can lead to a football pools win! Indeed rabbinic teaching is "you shalt not allow the sorcerer to live!" That is superstition, not faith. Superstition lives on and is fed by pseudo-miracles – magic! Faith grows by learning more and more how we can recognise God's presence and influence. Faith is the attempt to live in God's presence.

We look again at our text. Peter's shadow is a statement that faith still has a place. From the world's point of view Jesus had been killed – crucified – but faith sees the reality of his power being still at work. The possibility for the human spirit of Jesus teaching is as valid as ever – even in his followers' shadows!

It's a dull life in which the unexpected and unexplained does not occur. But it's a rich life when these events are not accidental but a revelation of God's love for us and his claims upon us. Maybe we should be trying to let Peter's shadow fall on us. After all it only has power because he received it from Jesus.

2 KINGS 2: 1-25

1. Now when the Lord was about to take Eli'jah up to heaven by a whirlwind, Eli'jah and Eli'sha were on their way from Gilgal.

2. And Eli'jah said to Eli'sha, "Tarry here, I pray you; for the Lord has sent me as far as Bethel." But Eli'sha said, "As the Lord lives, and as you yourself live, I will not leave you." So they went down to Bethel.

3. And the sons of the prophets who were in Bethel came out to Eli'sha, and said to him, "Do you know that today the Lord will take away your master from over you?" And he said, "Yes, I know it; hold your peace."

4. Eli'jah said to him, "Eli'sha, tarry here, I pray you; for the Lord has sent me to Jer'icho." But he said, "As the Lord lives, and as you yourself live, I will not leave you." So they came to Jericho.

5. The sons of the prophets who were at Jer'icho drew near to Eli'sha, and said to him, "Do you know that today the Lord will take away your master from over you?" And he answered, "Yes, I know it; hold your peace."

6. Then Eli'jah said to him, "Tarry here, I pray you; for the Lord has sent me to the Jordan." But he said, "As the Lord lives, and as you yourself live, I will not leave you." So the two of them went on.

7. Fifty men of the sons of the prophets also went, and stood at some distance from them, as they both were standing by the Jordan.

8. Then Eli'jah took his mantle, and rolled it up, and struck the water, and the water was parted to the one side and to the other, till the two of them could go over on dry ground.

9. When they had crossed, Eli'jah said to Eli'sha, "Ask what I shall do for you, before I am taken from you." And Eli'sha said, "I pray you, let me inherit a double share of your spirit."

10. And he said, "You have asked a hard thing; yet, if you see me as I am being taken from you, it shall be so for you; but if you do not see me, it shall not be so."

11. And as they still went on and talked, behold, a chariot of fire and horses of fire separated the two of them. And Eli'jah went up by a whirlwind into heaven.

12. And Eli'sha saw it and he cried, "My father, my father! the chariots of Israel and its horsemen!" And he saw him no more. Then he took hold of his own clothes and rent them in two pieces.

13. And he took up the mantle of Eli'jah that had fallen from him, and went back and stood on the bank of the Jordan.

14. Then he took the mantle of Eli'jah that had fallen from him, and struck the water, saying, "Where is the Lord, the God of Eli'jah?" And when he had struck the water, the water was parted to the one side and to the other; and Eli'sha went over.

15. Now when the sons of the prophets who were at Jer'icho saw him over against them, they said, "The spirit of Eli'jah rests on Eli'sha." And they came to meet him, and bowed to the ground before him.

16. And they said to him, "Behold now, there are with your servants fifty strong men; pray, let them go, and seek your master; it may be that the Spirit of the Lord has caught him up and cast him upon some mountain or into some valley." And he said, "You shall not send."

17. But when they urged him till he was ashamed, he said, "Send." They sent therefore fifty men; and for three days they sought him but did not find him.

18. And they came back to him, while he tarried at Jer'icho, and he said to them, "Did I not say to you, Do not go?"

19. Now the men of the city said to Eli'sha, "Behold, the situation of this city is pleasant, as my lord sees; but the water is bad, and the land is unfruitful."

20. He said, "Bring me a new bowl, and put salt in it." So they brought it to him.

21. Then he went to the spring of water and threw salt in it, and said, "Thus says the Lord, I have made this water wholesome; henceforth neither death nor miscarriage shall come from it."

22. So the water has been wholesome to this day, according to the word which Eli'sha spoke.

23. He went up from there to Bethel; and while he was going up on the way, some small boys came out of the city and jeered at him, saying, "Go up, you baldhead! Go up, you baldhead!"

24. And he turned around, and when he saw them, he cursed them in the name of the Lord. And two she-bears came out of the woods and tore forty-two of the boys.

25. From there he went on to Mount Carmel, and thence he returned to Samar'ia.

22.

"The Chariots of Israel and its horsemen."

There is a type of story which, I think, used to be more common than it is now. The Germans have a name for it. They call it BUBENMAERCHEN – "a little boy's story". It's a kind of cautionary story – 'look what will happen to you if you misbehave!' The whole idea was to frighten young boys into behaving themselves. I could comment on the psychology of this but I leave that to you to think about. However, there is a suggestion that the latter part of 2 Kings 2 is such a story. It certainly makes it more palatable to think of it as a story rather than have to reckon with a prophet of God, or indeed God himself coming along and sending out two she-bears to kill forty-two boys just because they were cheeky. We would soon have a world without young boys if this story was repeated in reality! Perhaps some parents in Old Testament days would read or tell this story to their offspring with an appropriate warning. But I'm fairly sure they would know there was more to it than just a fright for youngsters. Let's look at it in a bit more detail.

In Leviticus chapter 21 there are regulations about

who was suitable to be a priest, i.e. a servant of God. And it was ruled that since the priest was the one who made our offerings to God, and since these offerings had to be without blemish, it was only fitting that the priest himself should be without blemish. Private life conduct was important – the priest should not marry an impure woman. His hair should be properly cared for, and his hairdressing should be such that no loose hair can defile an offering by being loose. His limbs should be of equal length – no hunchback nor mutilations of the face. (I would add a note here of my own experience – when I was an assistant I had to help offer communion to people who worked in shipyards and factories. My mentor impressed on me the importance of presentation – do not offer communion with dirty fingernails – the men would notice and not appreciate it!) Perhaps the conduct of the ritual requires some kind of suitability on the part of the celebrant. It makes sense. It's when the act becomes pernickety that they become off-putting, or rules for the sake of rules. And this story highlights that. I think we all know that baldness is for many people just natural. But to the Jewish nit-picking rule-makers it was a feature to be understood as a criterion of fitness for office of priest. For such, forehead baldness was acceptable – it was deemed to be examined in the light of the "type" of baldness. Forehead baldness was considered reasonable – it was the result of pressure of the warrior's head-dress: or it was the result of scholarship – the mind worked so hard that it grew through the head, or it was the result of the poor diet of a slave. (It is worth noting that the Shetland baldness was considered to be due to a diet of too much fish and salt!) All this aside, the general consensus was that it was better not to be bald. The book of Isaiah tells us that baldness is a curse from God. Yet, here in 2 Kings 2 it is apparent that Elisha was bald – hence the small boys taunt. And, now we read that Elisha had just become God's prophet to the nation (how can that be? He was bald!) Thus, we can see that this story is becoming more subtle than just another example of a "little boy's story".

We are being told that immature people often judge by appearance only and in so doing fail to see the reality and thus fail to see when God is at work, and this failure leaves them unable to recognise the true prophet. And this little story about cheeky boys becomes a warning to us, not just boys. How do we recognise the working of God in our world? We have to see that there are some people who have a spiritual leadership quality – call them prophets, saints, blessèd, or whatever they have a deeper relationship with God than the rest of us – and this is what is meant by Elijah being taken up into heaven in a whirlwind – i.e. he was so close to God he did not have to die to be with him. Also, we learn from the story that to acquire such a gift as closeness to God required persistence and a willingness to trust. Three times in the story Elijah discourages Elisha from following him: but Elisha persists and he even persists when it does not seem to make sense; read the passage with a map in your hand and you'll find a very circuitous route – God's way is not easy and not always making our idea of sense. But if we persist even through obscurity the meaning does become clear.

I read a newspaper story of a fisherman who got caught in the rope holding the fishing nets. He, in his own words, struggled and "said a quick prayer." His prayer was a call for help for himself. Elisha's prayer was "for a double portion of your spirit." In Jewish terminology this is a prayer for the inheritance position of the first born – and in his case totally unselfish – Elisha was asking to be able to deal with all Elijah's difficulties – i.e. the problem of Jezebel and paganism. He was not praying for an easy life. He asked for nothing for himself. And, if we read on we find that his Godliness purifies polluted water and increases fertility.

Lastly, from this story we are shown a pointer to Jesus. Because of Elijah being taken up to Heaven in a whirlwind it was believed he would return to announce the coming of the Messiah – the saviour. This was deeply believed – the crowds wanted to know if John the Baptist was Elijah returned! And part of the difficulty they had in recognising Jesus was that they did not see Elijah. They had to learn that Jesus coming was not a miraculous event such as the coming again of a prophet, but was to be seen in Jesus himself. He made meaningful all their prophecies and he alone fulfilled the true relationship with God that the prophets reached for. It's not purifying water or overcoming the evil of a Jezebel – it's not living in such a way that little boys need a warning – it's the Gospel of love and in that love the discovery that this is truly God's way. 2 Kings 2 prepares us for this – but we look to Jesus to see its reality.

1 CORINTHIANS 13: 1-13

1. If I speak in the tongues of men and of angels, but have not love, I am a noisy gong or a clanging cymbal.

2. And if I have prophetic powers, and understand all mysteries and all knowledge, and if I have all faith, so as to remove mountains, but have not love, I am nothing.

3. If I give away all I have, and if I deliver my body to be burned, but have not love, I gain nothing.

4. Love is patient and kind; love is not jealous or boastful;

5. It is not arrogant or rude. Love does not insist on its own way; it is not irritable or resentful;

6. It does not rejoice at wrong, but rejoices in the right.

7. Love bears all things, believes all things, hopes all things, endures all things.

8. Love never ends; as for prophecies, they will pass away; as for tongues, they will cease; as for knowledge, it will pass away.

9. For our knowledge is imperfect and our prophecy is imperfect;

10. But when the perfect comes, the imperfect will pass away.

11. When I was a child, I spoke like a child, I thought like a child, I reasoned like a child; when I became a man, I gave up childish ways.

12. For now we see in a mirror dimly, but then face to face. Now I know in part; then I shall understand fully, even as I have been fully understood.

13. So faith, hope, love abide, these three; but the greatest of these is love.

23.

"The greatest of these is Love."

In the middle of the last century, when India was about to become self-governing, a group of Christian missionaries sought an appointment with Mahatma Ghandi to ask what role, if any, the Christian Church would have in the independent country. The Mahatma assured them that the Christian faith had much to offer and he went on to elaborate. "If you want your faith to serve India I would ask three things:

1. Try to live like Jesus, the founder of your faith.
2. Do not water down your faith, and
3. Practise love for that more than anything else is what your faith has to offer."

Let's look at each of these in turn.

(1) Try to live like Jesus. We see in the Gospels how Jesus often stands out from the crowd because he shares none of their prejudices and judgements. In a sentence, "Jesus is different!" And it is this difference that offers humanity, hope, and salvation from its often life-denying instincts – read again his

meeting with Zaccheus.

He not only makes Zaccheus feel wanted, he gives him the joy of being free from his slavery to cheating and overcharging – he gives him instead a new start and the happiness to be free from his past. "Try to live like Jesus." I recall when I worked for the Church in Ghana, in Trinity College. I had to take my son for his piano examination. We went to the University Music Department where they had sound-proof rooms. While my son was in the exam room I sat outside in the car with all the windows open for a bit of coolness. From where I was parked I could see one of the university ground staff digging a trench for a water pipe. He was diligently working at his task when the Music Department set about practising their drumming, their tom-toms. The rhythm of the tom-toms was not that of pick-axe swinging and I noticed the struggle the groundsman had keeping his swing going. After a few minutes of struggle he saw he was getting nowhere; so he threw his pick-axe aside and joined the rhythm of the drums with a dance! And there's a parable there. We must try to capture the rhythm of Jesus' life and his actions can be ours too. Try to be like Jesus, let him be the rhythm of our lives.

(2) Ghandi also said "Don't water down your faith." I find the phrase "practising Christian" difficult to understand. It seems to mean "he goes to Church." We all, I'm sure, know lots of people who go to Church, but they are capable of actions that don't seem to be very Christian; temptation can show the real character. When Trinity College was being built the main site was about 1¼ miles from a water

supply. The site of the college itself had a village behind it with no running water. The builders calculated that the cost of digging a trench for the water pipe depended on the size of pipe to be laid. The college needed a water supply that a three-inch pipe would carry – but a four-inch pipe would provide running water for the village as well. An offer was made to the villagers, that if they dug the trench the four-inch pipe could be used and it would not add to the building costs because the labour in digging the trench was the difference between the size of pipe.

Accordingly, an approach was made to the villagers and received a promise that they would discuss it. After a time there was a further approach which met with the response that it was being discussed. Now there is a point to be remembered here. It was the women who carried the water. The men were busy discussing. Suffice it to say the three-inch pipe was laid while the discussions went on. It was a year or two after this that my car was being serviced by one of the mechanics who lived in the village. He said that they were all upset because they had decided that they still wanted running water so they agreed to collect money every month until they reached the target. But the man who acted as treasurer had run away with the money. I pointed out to him that in Scotland we would have a banking system and signing a cheque would require at least two signatures. In this way there was a built-in safeguard. He looked at me, almost puzzled, and said this was the second person who had absconded with the money and they would just carry on again – and he then explained it – if they had the money as I said, it would not be fair – because he would not get his turn! The villagers were mostly "practising Christians" but when it came to their turn to collect the funds too many of them would fall to the temptation and "water down their faith!"

(3) Ghandi also said, "Practise love, for this more than anything else is what your religion has to offer the world. Practise love."

Abraham Lincoln was one of the greatest Presidents the USA has had and he was a fine Christian gentleman. I like the story of a trip he made with some of his staff. On the Sunday he went to Church and after the service a staff member asked him, "What did the minister preach about?"

Lincoln answered, "Sin." His companion then asked what the preacher said about sin. Lincoln answered, "He was agin it!"

But there is a better and very Christian story. Lincoln was attending a meeting of Congress and expected to be questioned. His staff, as always, had prepared as many answers as they could. But to one question the answer was entirely and ridiculously wrong and Lincoln was laughed at. After the meeting he called on the staff member who gave him his answer – quite a young man who had worked for a time with Lincoln. Lincoln met him and asked, "How long have you worked for me now?"

"A few years," was the answer.

Lincoln then asked, "In that time how many answers have you prepared for me?"

The reply came, "Over 100."

Lincoln looked at him and said, "How remiss of me not to thank you for all the times your support has been excellent – forgive me for being so impolite."

That is love! Lincoln didn't even mention the earlier mistake. This was a Christian soul at work – and that young man would have his confidence fully restored and a loyalty firmly built. Love is a word that is made to cover many different meanings. But Christian love is deeper than all the rest put together.

Try to live like Jesus

Don't water down your faith

Practise love

That's Jesus' agenda for Christians and someday hopefully to the world.

EZEKIEL 33: 1-20

1. The word of the Lord came to me:

2. "Son of man, speak to your people and say to them, If I bring the sword upon a land, and the people of the land take a man from among them, and make him their watchman;

3. And if he sees the sword coming upon the land and blows the trumpet and warns the people;

4. Then if any one who hears the sound of the trumpet does not take warning, and the sword comes and takes him away, his blood shall be upon his own head.

5. He heard the sound of the trumpet, and did not take warning; his blood shall be upon himself. But if he had taken warning, he would have saved his life.

6. But if the watchman sees the sword coming and does not blow the trumpet, so that the people are not warned, and the sword comes, and takes any one of them; that man is taken away in his iniquity, but his blood I will require at the watchman's hand.

7. "So you, son of man, I have made a watchman for the house of Israel; whenever you hear a word from my mouth, you shall give them warning from me.

8. If I say to the wicked, O wicked man, you shall surely die, and you do not speak to warn the wicked to turn from his way, that wicked man shall die in his iniquity, but his blood I will require at your hand.

9. But if you warn the wicked to turn from his way, and he does not turn from his way; he shall die in his iniquity, but you will have saved your life.

10. "And you, son of man, say to the house of Israel, Thus have you said: 'Our transgressions and our sins are upon us, and we waste away because of them; how then can we live?'

11. Say to them, As I live, says the Lord God, I have no pleasure in the death of the wicked, but that the wicked turn from his way and live; turn back, turn back from your evil ways; for why will you die, O house of Israel?

12. And you, son of man, say to your people, The righteousness of the righteous shall not deliver him when he transgresses; and as for the wickedness of the wicked, he shall not fall by it when he turns from his wickedness; and the righteous shall not be able to live by his righteousness when he sins.

13. Though I say to the righteous that he shall surely live, yet if he trusts in his righteousness and commits iniquity, none of his righteous deeds shall be remembered; but in the iniquity that he has committed he shall die.

14. Again, though I say to the wicked, 'You shall surely die,' yet if he turns from his sin and does what is lawful and right,

15. If the wicked restores the pledge, gives back what he has taken by robbery, and walks in the statutes of life, committing no iniquity; he shall surely live, he shall not die.

16. None of the sins that he has committed shall be remembered against him; he has done what is lawful and right, he shall surely live.

17. "Yet your people say, 'The way of the Lord is not just'; when it is their own way that is not just.

18. When the righteous turns from his righteousness, and commits iniquity, he shall die for it.

19. And when the wicked turns from his wickedness, and does what is lawful and right, he shall live by it.

20. Yet you say, 'The way of the Lord is not just.' O house of Israel, I will judge each of you according to his ways."

24.

"The righteousness of the righteous shall not believe him when he transgresses and as for the wickedness of the wicked, he shall not fall by it when he turns from his wickedness."

I imagine we have all heard the expression "a practising Christian". We usually hear it on TV or radio in a report about a person currently in the news about something they have done – both in good and bad contexts – and to be truthful I'm not always sure of what it means. It seems sometimes to mean nothing more than they go to Church – often – sometimes – regularly? Is Church attendance a criterion for being a practising Christian? It would be nice to think that Church attendance results in recognisable Christian conduct. But does it?

I recall a situation in a parish near where I used to work. A small business man was having difficulty in getting his books to balance and he knew full well he was to be declared bankrupt. He drove his car into the local garage and had it filled with petrol and told the garage owner (not a big firm but a family group trying to make ends meet) to fit new tyres as the old ones were nearing their useful date – and just to put the tyres on the business account. He knew full well that the garage owner would be lucky if he received 10p in the pound when the business was closed down. The garage owner was a fellow Rotarian. And our business man was a Church member who sang in the choir and rarely missed a service. Would you describe him as a "practising" Christian? I don't think that was what the garage owner or his fellow Rotarians thought when the incident became public knowledge!

Over and against this I had a situation in a parish where I used to work. It was Christian Aid week and the ladies of the congregation duly posted envelopes for contributions through the household doors and promised to collect them at a later date. One lady came to me a bit perplexed and sought my help. She had put her envelope through Miss McInnes's door and on collecting it found that it contained a £5 note. She knew well that Miss McInnes could not afford that and also her eyesight was not what it once was – so she thought a mistake had been made. I took the envelope and the £5 note and said I'd see to it. I duly went to Miss McInnes's door. She had for most of her working life served as a primary schoolteacher at one of the Church's missionary stations in East Africa. And now in her old age she was living in a small tenement flat and on a Church pension was struggling to make ends meet. I handed her the envelope and contents and offered to take the £5 and let her replace it with ten shillings. She looked at me –

and I still remember the saintly nature of that look – and said that it had been a mistake but the reason must have been because the African children needed the money more than her and that God, by her mistake, was reminding her of her Christian duty – and she emphatically refused to take the £5 back. I felt humbled! I was in the presence of a saint! And by the way, Miss McInnes didn't attend Church very regularly. The tenement stairs and the walk up the hill was now too much for her to manage!

Who was the practising Christian? The man who sang in the choir and defrauded his fellow Rotarian or the one who rarely managed to Church but rejoiced in her poverty that she could still help with God's work? The question doesn't invite an answer – but a question – how do you get to being a saint from being a stinker? (And by the way, I was very proud of my congregation. Miss McInnes received many knocks on her door for the next few weeks only to find no-one was there. But on the doorstep was a packet of tea – a box of eggs – a tin of soup – a jar of coffee – a packet of sugar – a loaf of bread and jar of jam, etc. "Cast thy bread upon the waters." I was proud of my congregation with a tear in my eye!)

So how do you get from being a stinker to being a saint – who is the practising Christian? We know the answer to the second part of the question – but first – HOW? We turn to St Peter – Peter the rock – the one who was given "the keys of the Kingdom". Peter who was the first to recognise Jesus – "Thou art the Christ, the Son of the living God." This was the Simon renamed by Jesus as Peter – "the rock" – this was Peter who was symbolically given "the keys of the Kingdom." Yet this was Peter who on the night of his arrest denied all knowledge of Jesus. Was Jesus wrong in calling him a rock? What we learn here is that Jesus loves us not only for what we are but also for what we can be. And it's interesting that the one you would think would never falter is the very one who does. I don't think that we are meant to realise Peter's frailty – but rather Peter's failure to recognise just how much Jesus was the son of God. It was a crisis of faith, not of strength, i.e. physical strength – who can doubt that from the ROCK? We are being told that Jesus not only loves us for what we are, but what we can be.

This passage in Ezekial: "The righteousness of the righteous shall not deliver him when he transgresses and as for the wickedness of the wicked he shall not fall by it when he turns from his wickedness." What Ezekial means is that even the righteous is capable of falling – and the wicked is capable of doing good. It is not a particular act that determines what we are really – it's our whole demeanour – our personal acceptance of God's will for us for the whole of life – not just when it's going badly.

How do I get from being a stinker to being a saint? By realising that God's requirement of us is that we live by Jesus' agenda – even when it's not to our advantage – even when it hurts – but then, that is truly what being a "practising" Christian should mean. Not just when it's convenient but all the time.

LUKE 19: 11-27

11. And as they heard these things, he added and spake a parable, because he was nigh to Jerusalem, and because they thought that the kingdom of God should immediately appear.

12. He said therefore, A certain nobleman went into a far country to receive for himself a kingdom, and to return.

13. And he called his ten servants, and delivered them ten pounds, and said unto them, Occupy till I come.

14. But his citizens hated him, and sent a message after him, saying, We will not have this man to reign over us.

15. And it came to pass, that when he was returned, having received the kingdom, then he commanded these servants to be called unto him, to whom he had given the money, that he might know how much every man had gained by trading.

16. Then came the first, saying, Lord, thy pound hath gained ten pounds.

17. And he said unto him, Well, thou good servant: because thou hast been faithful in a very little, have thou authority over ten cities.

18. And the second came, saying, Lord, thy pound hath gained five pounds.

19. And he said likewise to him, Be thou also over five cities.

20. And another came, saying, Lord, behold, here is thy pound, which I have kept laid up in a napkin:

21. For I feared thee, because thou art an austere man: thou takest up that thou layedst not down, and reapest that thou didst not sow.

22. And he saith unto him, Out of thine own mouth will I

judge thee, thou wicked servant. Thou knewest that I was an austere man, taking up that I laid not down, and reaping that I did not sow:

23. Wherefore then gavest not thou my money into the bank, that at my coming I might have required mine own with usury?

24. And he said unto them that stood by, Take from him the pound, and give it to him that hath ten pounds.

25. (And they said unto him, Lord, he hath ten pounds.)

26. For I say unto you, That unto every one which hath shall be given; and from him that hath not, even that he hath shall be taken away from him.

27. But those mine enemies, which would not that I should reign over them, bring hither, and slay them before me.

25.

"Trade with these till I come."

Some time ago a European football club bought a player from Brazil for £5,000,000. The player actually only cost the team £1,250,000. The reason for this was that the Brazil economy had fallen badly into debt. In fact, the management of the economy had been taken over by the world bank. Knowing this, the finance director of the football club bought £5,000,000 in Brazilian currency, and it cost £1,250,000. A big saving to the club indeed. Of necessity the Brazilian currency had been devalued and to replace it with an exchangeable currency it was sold off to recover as much as possible. So the European football team got their player on the cheap (sic!). But, the way international finance works, the result for Brazil was further inflation. Consequently the poor Brazilian people had to pay more for their sausages! This was a shrewd piece of trading. It was perfectly legal and probably the club accountant was congratulated and maybe even got a bonus. Legal? Yes – but fair? When Jesus told the parable about the king who gave his servants money and the instruction, "Trade with these till I come," do you think this football team's conduct of the transfer payment would have met with his approval? It is a truth in worldly matters that what is legal is not always fair. We really have to ask ourselves in all our dealings whether or not we think Jesus would approve. And, frankly, more often than not we are happy enough just to be legal – never mind the fairness.

Let us then look at this parable. It is unique among the parables so much so that a number of scholars suggest we should not call it a parable but instead call it an allegory, because it appears to be based on an actual event. When Herod the great died he divided his Kingdom into three, each part to one of his natural heirs. Indeed it is recorded that one of his heirs, Archelaus, actually sailed to Rome to persuade Caesar Augustus to confirm him in his Kingdom, but Caesar did confirm him as requested but refused him the right to use the title 'King'. Instead he allowed him to be called 'Ethnarch', i.e. 'ruler of the race'. And while Archelaus was in Rome fifty spokesmen for the Jews were sent to tell Caesar that they did not want to be governed by Herod's family anymore. So what Jesus is saying is that the Kingdom of Heaven will be like being ruled by a foreign ruler who does not value the things you value, who will not see as important the things you see as important, whose tradition and customs are different from yours. Put simply this means that in the Kingdom of Heaven a different understanding of morality will apply. However, the more we understand the principles that Jesus wants us to live by, the more we should learn to be glad. Glad, yes, because we won't have it on our conscience that we made life harder for the ordinary folk in a poor country. Not for us the unfairness of much of our commerce. Bank manipulation of exchange rates that lead to massive bonuses – but which really, is theft. Not for us the overseas bank accounts that are used to avoid paying tax. Followers of Jesus have his idea of fairness. None of us like paying tax but when we see how many people are losers when we don't do our fair share – then surely we think again.

It was St Paul, who as so often, could put this concisely – "You are no longer strangers or foreigners but fellow citizens with the saints and of the Kingdom of Heaven." This is his definition of a Christian – a fellow citizen with the saints. The Christian faith sees us in this way. I think, and I'm sure you will join me – it's better to practise being a fellow citizen than to perpetuate legal unfairness.

PSALM 8: 1-9

1. O Lord, our Lord, how excellent is thy name in all the earth! who hast set thy glory above the heavens.

2. Out of the mouth of babes and sucklings hast thou ordained strength because of thine enemies, that thou mightest still the enemy and the avenger.

3. When I consider thy heavens, the work of thy fingers, the moon and the stars, which thou hast ordained;

4. What is man, that thou art mindful of him? and the son of man, that thou visitest him?

5. For thou hast made him a little lower than the angels, and hast crowned him with glory and honour.

6. Thou madest him to have dominion over the works of thy hands; thou hast put all things under his feet:

7. All sheep and oxen, yea, and the beasts of the field;

8. The fowl of the air, and the fish of the sea, and whatsoever passeth through the paths of the seas.

9. O Lord our Lord, how excellent is thy name in all the earth!

26.

"What is man that thou art mindful of him?"

Sometimes it is a good exercise to see how our faith is regarded by other people – especially if the person concerned is someone we respect, someone who is serious. Such a person is the late Sir Patrick Moore. I'm sure we all remember his programme "The Sky at Night." He came over as the man with the monocle who talked at 100mph! He was fascinated with astronomy and was recognised as having a strong and serious interest in knowledge of the stars. Indeed it was his mapping of the moon that the American astronauts used to plan their moon walks. His expertise was well recognised – an MBE, an OBE, and a Knighthood. This is all the more remarkable when we learn that he never finished his schooling because of ill-health in his youth. This just makes his achievements the more remarkable. He was an R.A.F. navigator officer in the war at the age of 17! His mapping interests made him a natural for this task. Also in his younger years he was engaged to a young lady "Lorna". Lorna, alas, was killed in an air raid and Sir Patrick to the end of his days could not forgive the Germans. He was like that! And his black and white look at the world made him a scourge of bureaucrats. He didn't hesitate to say what he thought. This side of him made him a critic of any public figure. He was in turn president and secretary of the astronomy international committee. His story of their meeting in Argentina as he tells it in his autobiography is an example of what he most disliked in his experience of some public figures. President Menem of Argentina was invited as a matter of courtesy. He came to the opening ceremony – but only on condition that there would be a semi-circle with his chair in the middle position. Then in his opening speech which on the whole wasn't bad, he ended it by remarking that he knew very well the importance of Astrology!

We've spent quite a time looking at Sir Patrick but that's deliberate. We had to assure ourselves that he was someone of substance whose opinion is worth listening to. So we now turn to see what he thinks of religion and in particular, Christianity.

At one point in his astronomical career he went to Northern Ireland for a few months to help establish an astronomy centre. He had been in England as a Boy Scout and went on to be a leader. So in Northern Ireland he went to a scout troupe to offer his services.

He was greeted with the question – "Are you a catholic or a protestant?"

His reply was, "Why does this matter?" And his comment in his book is – they should lock up all the bishops and bang Church leaders' heads together and lock them in a room and tell them to sort things out. The religious divide in that country was and still is a disgrace to Christian faith – and whenever and wherever such divisiveness is found it is to be seen as a betrayal of the Gospel of love and definitely not a part of Jesus' agenda for his world. It certainly was enough to put Sir Patrick off. We must examine ourselves and our Churches and ask whether we are an acceptable presentation of what Jesus stood for. Feelings and loyalties run deep. But when they take the place of loyalty to Jesus and the Gospel, we must think again.

Another matter Sir Patrick raised was his reply to the question quite often put in a letter – it asked, "Do you read the Bible?"

His answer was, "I do not read science fiction."

Here he indicates where the Church often fails, in particular among the fundamentalists – we expect the Bible to be read and believed literally. In our generation with all the advancements in science and knowledge of how the world came to be and how we ourselves have developed the Bible stories are treated as science fiction. In some places in the USA today there are frequent protests at school gates to try to ensure that "creationism" is taught as well as evolution. This puts many people beyond faith. The Bible contains great stories to help our faith and they all can be interpreted in a way that helps faith to grow rather than put them off. Incidentally Sir Patrick knew his Bible and had read it. He even has a little fun with it – he purported to be able to show from the tests that Jesus was a good golfer – even to the extent that we're told he sometimes had a bad stroke for which the text is "and some fell on stony ground!" (I know that feeling.) I think Jesus himself would laugh at this kind of fun being made of a story.

A very interesting point is Sir Patrick's notion about death. Many of our modern scientists are of the opinion that our death is the end as far as we are concerned. But not Sir Patrick. He was so impressed by wonder and magnificence of the universe that he had to say – it is all so wonderful that "if my death is the end as far as I am concerned then this universe is pointless and it's just too magnificent to be pointless – so it will not be the end for us."

One last thought, Sir Patrick was quite passionately against fox hunting with hounds. The thought of a living fox terrorised into running for its life and then being caught and ripped to shreds for fun – it was a sport, after all. Such a thought appalled him. He wrote to three different Archbishops of Canterbury to ask them to use their good offices to end this brutal cruelty. In each case he received a polite response but no indication that they would take an opportunity to speak out against this barbaric practice. Sir Patrick comments, "If this is Christianity, give me paganism every time."

Here was an honest and serious man who would have been a great asset to the Church – but it would have to be a Church that worked to Jesus' agenda. That's the challenge to us – do we, and do our Churches conduct our affairs in such a way to enrich our faith by accepting the criticisms of the Sir Patricks of this world?

MATTHEW 28: 1-10

1. Now after the sabbath, toward the dawn of the first day of the week, Mary Mag'dalene and the other Mary went to see the sepulchre.

2. And behold, there was a great earthquake; for an angel of the Lord descended from heaven and came and rolled back the stone, and sat upon it.

3. His appearance was like lightning, and his raiment white as snow.

4. And for fear of him the guards trembled and became like dead men.

5. But the angel said to the women, "Do not be afraid; for I know that you seek Jesus who was crucified.

6. He is not here; for he has risen, as he said. Come, see the place where he lay.

7. Then go quickly and tell his disciples that he has risen from the dead, and behold, he is going before you to Gal'ilee; there you will see him. Lo, I have told you."

8. So they departed quickly from the tomb with fear and great joy, and ran to tell his disciples.

9. And behold, Jesus met them and said, "Hail!" And they came up and took hold of his feet and worshiped him.

10. Then Jesus said to them, "Do not be afraid; go and tell my brethren to go to Gal'ilee, and there they will see me."

27.

"He is not here, for he has risen as he said."

THE RESURRECTION IS A NOW EVENT.

The Christian faith is a resurrection faith: there can be no doubt about that. But how to understand what the Resurrection is or means is subject to many suggestions. The first thing to notice is that no one saw the resurrection – what was seen was an empty tomb. And this has given rise to imaginative interpretations – e.g. friends took his body away and gave him a decent burial. But there is no evidence to support this. We do not get a resurrection faith by arguing about what happened on the first Easter Day. "He is not here," is what St Matthew says. Some people are prepared to say that believing in a physical resurrection is a requirement of all who wish to call themselves Christians. If we take that line then I'm sure we will lose a lot of Church members. I've had it said to me often – "I believe in the Christian message but I cannot take all the miracles." And this stance receives support from many devout theologians. Rudolf Bultmann in the 19th century dismissed a literal interpretation with the words: "what kind of historical idea can that be – the resurrection of the dead" and he goes on to seek for a meaning for faith other than a literal belief. David Jenkins, when he was Bishop of Durham, hit the newspapers by labelling a literal belief in the resurrection as believing that God does "conjuring tricks with bones!" The late Glasgow University Professor Ronald Gregor Smith wrote simply that the early Church chose the wrong model for what they wanted to say by choosing the Resurrection. We have to look at an understanding of what they meant by so choosing.

It is important to recognise that these scholars are all devout Christian people. They are not trying to deny a central item of the Christian faith – rather they are seeking to remove what for many is a stumbling block and help to make it helpful and very relevant in our everyday living. Harry Williams, the Cambridge scholar, gives a fair illustration of this. He sees it as the discovery of a deeper meaning. An artist who paints for a living, tires of mere painting but discovers he can use his art as a means of presenting a vision that makes people think more deeply – that, he says, is resurrection. The elderly couple whose relationship has become habit develop a new relationship which is less greedy, more stable, a discovery of true one-ness. This is resurrection. He even suggests that a freed slave having a night on the tiles, by doing the forbidden is taking a step towards true resurrection. It is a brave Christian theologian who can see a night on the tiles in a positive context, but that just shows how powerful a thought through meaning of the resurrection is – it can even make the negative positive! It is a call for us to examine our living and with God's help to eliminate the negative and assert the positive! We all have known people with an ample amount of money who are enslaved by it and allowed it to become life's goal – equally we have met people who don't know where the next meal is coming from but still manage to be free from worry and meet life's experience positively. Who, of these, is nearer to resurrection faith?

The ten commandments, the foundation for so much of civilisation, have to be examined in this light. In fact, the ten commandments as we meet them in the book of Exodus are two commandments and eight prohibitions! It is quite commonplace as a result of these commandments to judge Christianity by them. I can't count the number of times I've had it said to me – the Church is always against enjoying yourself! Don't do this – don't do that. But viewed in the light of the resurrection faith, these prohibitions should be seen as challenging obstacles to fulfilment – with the resurrection even a negative has a positive connotation! The ten commandments seek to help us avoid those things that inhibit rather than enable us to be what God wants us to be. Put bluntly, if we see the commandments as negative we have failed to see their religious meaning!

Believing in the Resurrection as a miracle that happened long ago, and we have to swallow hard and accept it, fails in two ways. It reduces the Christian faith to an Alice through the looking glass "believing ten impossible things before breakfast!" And it robs it of its positive meaning for faith today. The resurrection is a "now" event and only as such does it bring to life the power and insight of Jesus!

On Friday June 19, 2015, there was a report in the

newspapers of the tragic death of David Woodall, aged 35. He was a police constable in Edmonton, Alberta, and was shot on duty trying to arrest a suspect. He and his wife had left Manchester nine years prior to this hoping for a better lifestyle. They had two children aged six and four. The newspapers carried a photograph of the procession of his police colleagues. There were literally thousands at his funeral and the police procession was so large that it could not show the whole parade. It was something special – a parade of sorrow and support. Claire Woodall is reported as saying, "There are really no words great enough to express my love and gratitude to the city of Edmonton. You have shown so much love and support to myself and my family. We will be forever grateful. I am lucky to call Edmonton my home. Thank you." This is the experience of resurrection. Amor vincit omnia – as the Church in an earlier generation expressed, "LOVE CONQUERS ALL." For a young widow still in the rawness of her loss to be able to speak in this way shows just how powerful love is – "resurrection powerful". Love strengthens and supports.

In a much less dramatic way, but still important, Martin Buber, the Jewish philosopher and theologian, tells a nice simple story. He boarded a taxi in New York and after the journey went into his hotel. To sign the book, he went into his pocket for his glasses only to discover they were missing. Elderly as he was, his glasses were vital. Not too long later he saw a man entering in the doorway and as he got nearer he recognised his taxi driver. The driver gave him his glasses and Buber embraced him and said, "Good boy." That was a resurrection moment, not just a triviality. An old man's need enabled the driver to ignore the hustle and bustle of the city and its traffic chaos (and his own need to keep his taxi busy to earn a living). Jesus can and does rise when we allow him – even in the trivia of daily life. What a wonderful doctrine the resurrection is!

THE RESURRECTION IS A NOW EVENT.

Sea of blue: Members of the Edmonton Police Service follow the hearse carrying the coffin of slain Edmonton Police officer, Constable Daniel Woodall, during the Regimental Funeral Procession in Edmonton Wednesday.

(Photograph and caption courtesy of Dailymail.com – published 00:19, 18th June, 2015)

MATTHEW 7: 15-29

15. "Beware of false prophets, who come to you in sheep's clothing but inwardly are ravenous wolves.

16. You will know them by their fruits. Are grapes gathered from thorns, or figs from thistles?

17. So, every sound tree bears good fruit, but the bad tree bears evil fruit.

18. A sound tree cannot bear evil fruit, nor can a bad tree bear good fruit.

19. Every tree that does not bear good fruit is cut down and thrown into the fire.

20. Thus you will know them by their fruits.

21. "Not every one who says to me, 'Lord, Lord,' shall enter the kingdom of heaven, but he who does the will of my Father who is in heaven.

22. On that day many will say to me, 'Lord, Lord, did we not prophesy in your name, and cast out demons in your name, and do many mighty works in your name?'

23. And then will I declare to them, 'I never knew you; depart from me, you evildoers.'

24. "Every one then who hears these words of mine and does them will be like a wise man who built his house upon the rock;

25. And the rain fell, and the floods came, and the winds blew and beat upon that house, but it did not fall, because it had been founded on the rock.

26. And every one who hears these words of mine and does not do them will be like a foolish man who built his house upon the sand;

27. And the rain fell, and the floods came, and the winds blew and beat against that house, and it fell; and great was the fall of it."

28. And when Jesus finished these sayings, the crowds were astonished at his teaching,

29. For he taught them as one who had authority, and not as their scribes.

28.

"Not everyone who says to me, 'Lord, Lord' shall enter the Kingdom of Heaven, but he who does the will of my Father who is in heaven."

Allow me to tell you of an experience of a minister in a small country parish. He was approached by a colleague in one of our cities to try to help a family that needed a place of safety. There was some neighbourly problem which was accompanied by smoke bombs through the door of their house and the children were quite seriously concerned. The country minister approached a primary school head teacher to try to arrange schooling for them. The head teacher was a self-proclaimed Christian who made sure the children knew their Bible stories and learned to sing some hymns. On the minister's request his reply was not one of willingness for threatened children nor sympathetic in any way. He stated that they would not be treated like other children – he would not give them jotters but sheets of paper and they would have to supply their own writing instruments. The minister went to another small school head mistress. Her Christianity consisted in going to Church with the children at Christmas and the End of Year service. She welcomed the three children with open arms and made sure they were in no way made to feel different – they were made to feel as normal as possible. "Not everyone who says to me 'Lord, Lord' but he who does the will of my Father." I have no doubt which of these two head teachers would meet Jesus' criteria of doing God's will.

I'm sure we all know of experiences like this. An interesting study in human behaviour was published in 2011 entitled "When the children came home" (authoress Julie Summers). It is a look at children who were evacuated during the war and their experiences – good and bad. There is the story of two sisters placed with a Welsh farmer and his wife. They began by burning all the children's clothes and dressing them in cast-offs. They shaved their hair to the bare scalp – and told them they had brought vermin from London and had to be made clean. It wasn't a good start to a relationship. There was the Roman Catholic family who had the care of a Methodist family and told them they were going to Hell unless they took Mass! On returning home they resumed their Methodist faith – but one had liked the Mass so much he committed to Catholicism – not to the family's delight! There were also cases of child abuse. But quite a number of the bad experiences came from overzealous Christian homes. But, to my mind, one stands out and that is a single man who didn't believe in the Church and wasn't sure about God – but he became an honorary "uncle" to a Jewish family. He learned their Jewish practices and food and joined in them with the children. He fasted with them on Yom Kippur – but one year he forgot and had bacon for breakfast and endured a raging thirst for the rest of the day. He was sad on V.E. Day because he was going to lose their company – and he visited them in their home as long as he was able. He sent money for wedding presents and left them a legacy in his will. Sheila said of him, "Uncle Harry was not sure about God but he was the truest Christian I have ever met." – "He who does the work of my Father."

And then there's Malala. The girl the Islamic Taliban tried to kill. She went public against them and challenged their orthodoxy in saying the Koran contains no woman's name. She pointed out it mentions Mary – but apparently that's just to show Jesus was born of a human. She recalls walking through a shopping mall and seeing men with guns. "I was terrified though I said nothing. I told myself, Malala, you have already faced death. This is your second life. Don't be afraid – if you are afraid you can't move forward." At the Kaaba they prayed for peace in Pakistan and for girls' education. She has received awards from round the world (America, India, France, Spain, Italy and Austria) and has been awarded the Nobel Peace Prize. It is people like that who can bring closer relationships between the religions of the world and I am sure Jesus would count her as among those who do the will of the Father.

And in 2012 a book was published that is both heart-rending and inspiring – *Always By My Side* by Christina Schmid. It tells of her relationship and marriage to Olaf (Oz) Schmid. Neither Christina nor Oz had a church background. In fact they could drink too much and generally speaking frequently behaved in a way that would make many people – not just Churchy – say, "Tut, tut!" Oz was a bomb disposal expert and fully knew the dangers of his job and the risks involved, particularly with I.E.Ds (improvised explosive devices). These were explosive bombs that would be planted in places where they would explode when vehicles passed or groups of soldiers marched by them. Oz was a staff sergeant and was one of the army's top men in the field. He frequently told his adopted son Laird (Christina had Laird before she married Oz) that his dad was a soldier who did not kill people but tried to save them. It was a job of immense pressure.

Ordinary explosives were made to a pattern and so, with extreme care, could be defused. But the improvised bombs were unpredictable and followed no pattern. And Oz felt the pressure. In Afghanistan at the time many such devices were in use. Oz was due leave to take the pressure off but was called back early as there was so much to be done. He indicated to Christina that he was unsure of his future and, indeed, instructed her how she was to cope with his death. And he did indeed die doing his job – he had a premonition – but refused to give in as so many other lives were at risk. He was awarded the George Cross for his bravery – he put others before his own life. Christina, for her deportment in doing all as Oz suggested and attended to his funeral – she was awarded the Elizabeth Cross. She has done much to make his name known and the nature of his work. She gave the eulogy at his funeral and has gone on to work at "tickets for troops" – a chance for soldiers and service personal to see shows affordably. At the end of Oz's funeral service the congregation rose and sang "Thine be the Glory". A Christian praise from a hero and not a particularly churchy man — "He who does the work of my Father."

A last thought — a book by Sally Magnusson — *Where Memory Goes* about her mother's Alzheimer's. The trials and problems are well known and very trying. But there's a sentence that says it all. People think that an Alzheimer's victim in the family is a burden, but Sally writes: "Where there is love there is no burden."

Not everyone who says "Lord, Lord" — but he who responds to need, not seeing it as a burden — because he knows the Jesus Agenda of letting love conquer prejudice, fear and the hurt of sacrifice. Jesus' Agenda is always responding with love.

Printed in Great Britain
by Amazon